ENGLISH
FOR EVERYONE
JUNIOR
BEGINNER'S COURSE
PRACTICE BOOK

FREE AUDIO
website and app

www.dkefe.com/junior/us

Author

Ben Ffrancon Davies is a freelance writer and translator. He writes textbooks and study guides on a wide range of subjects including ELT, history, and literature. He also works on general nonfiction books for children and adults. Ben studied Medieval and Modern Languages at the University of Oxford, and has taught English in France and Spain.

Course consultant

Susannah Reed is an experienced author and educational consultant, specializing in Primary ELT materials. She has taught in Spain and the UK and has worked in educational publishing for over 20 years, as both a publisher and a writer of ELT course books for children around the world.

Language consultant

Professor Susan Barduhn is an English-language teacher, teacher trainer, and author, who has contributed to numerous publications. She has been President of the International Association of Teachers of English as a Foreign Language, and an adviser to the British Council and the US State Department. She is currently a professor at the School of International Training in Vermont.

ENGLISH
FOR EVERYONE
JUNIOR
BEGINNER'S COURSE
PRACTICE BOOK

FREE AUDIO
website and app

www.dkefe.com/junior/us

Senior Editor Ben Ffrancon Davies
Senior Art Editor Amy Child
Illustrators Amy Child, Dan Crisp
Managing Editor Carine Tracanelli
Managing Art Editor Anna Hall
Senior Production Editor Andy Hilliard
Production Editor Gillian Reid
Senior Production Controllers Samantha Cross, Jude Crozier
Jacket Design Development Manager Sophia MTT
Senior Jacket Designer Surabhi Wadhwa-Gandhi
Jacket Designer Juhi Sheth
Senior Jackets Coordinator Priyanka Sharma-Saddi
DTP Designer Rakesh Kumar
Publisher Andrew Macintyre
Associate Publishing Director Liz Wheeler
Art Director Karen Self
Publishing Director Jonathan Metcalf

This American boxset edition, 2024
First American Edition, 2022
Published in the United States by DK Publishing
a Division of Penguin Random House LLC
1745 Broadway, 20th Floor, New York, NY 10019

Copyright © 2022, 2024
Dorling Kindersley Limited
24 25 26 27 10 9 8 7 6 5 4 3 2 1
001–340278–Jun/2024

All rights reserved.
Without limiting the rights under the copyright reserved above, no part of this publication may be reproduced, stored in or introduced into a retrieval system, or transmitted, in any form, or by any means (electronic, mechanical, photocopying, recording, or otherwise), without the prior written permission of the copyright owner. Published in Great Britain by Dorling Kindersley Limited

A catalog record for this book
is available from the Library of Congress.
Boxset ISBN 978-0-5938-4226-3
Book ISBN 978-0-7440-2846-1

DK books are available at special discounts when purchased in bulk for sales promotions, premiums, fund-raising, or educational use. For details, contact: DK Publishing Special Markets, 1745 Broadway, 20th Floor, New York, NY 10019
SpecialSales@dk.com

Printed and bound in China

www.dk.com

This book was made with Forest Stewardship Council™ certified paper – one small step in DK's commitment to a sustainable future. Learn more at www.dk.com/uk/information/sustainability

Contents

	About the course	6
1	My friends	10
2	At school	16
3	Our classroom	24
4	My things	30
5	Our favorite animals	38
6	This is my family	46
7	This is my room	54
8	Review: This is me	62
9	At the fair	64
10	Our pets	72

11	My body	80
12	Our town	88
13	My home	96
14	Review: Where I live	104
15	On the farm	106
16	Sports	114
17	At the food market	124
18	At the toy store	132
19	Our hobbies	140
20	Review: What I like	148
21	Our party clothes	150
22	Our day at the beach	158
23	Lunchtime	166
24	At the park	174
25	My day	182
26	Review: Me and my day	192

Handwriting guide	194
Answers	199
Acknowledgments	224

About the course

English for Everyone Junior: Beginner's Practice Book is a companion to the *English for Everyone Junior: Beginner's Course*. The course book is divided into 26 units—each with its own theme—and the practice book mirrors that structure. There is audio for all the units.

Our characters
A group of six friends—Maria, Sofia, Ben, Andy, Sara, and Max help you practice language in a natural and friendly way.

Unit structure
Each practice unit starts with a scene that presents the vocabulary taught in the corresponding course book unit. The child then practices this vocabulary along with the grammar rules they learned in that unit of the course book.

1 New vocabulary
The illustrated scene helps the child practice the vocabulary, as they listen to each word and write it in the correct space.

2 Vocabulary practice
There is more vocabulary practice. The child might be asked to match vocabulary to pictures or spell individual words.

3 Grammar practice
Each unit then practices the grammar rules taught in the corresponding course book unit while also studying vocabulary.

4 Grammar practice
More grammar is practiced. Many units also have a song to help learn new grammar and vocabulary.

Audio

English for Everyone Junior: Beginner's Practice Book features extensive supporting audio resources. Listening to and repeating the audio recordings will help the child master the pronunciation and stress patterns of English, as well as help them to cement new language in their memory.

Register at www.dkefe.com/junior/us to access the audio materials for free. Each file can be played, paused, and repeated as often as you like.

All vocabulary scenes, songs, and listening exercises have accompanying audio. Clicking on the corresponding number on the app will play the relevant audio file.

Most exercises have accompanying audio. After completing an exercise, the child should listen to the correct answers and then repeat them out loud.

FREE AUDIO
website and app

www.dkefe.com/junior/us

Review units

Four review units provide the child with a chance to read a text incorporating vocabulary and grammar from recent units. The child then writes a personalized answer based on this text.

Handwriting guide

The book includes a guide explaining how to form each letter of the English alphabet. The child has space to practice the formation of each letter.

Answers

At the back of the book, answers to all the exercises are clearly presented. Key information is sometimes shown in bold to make it easier to grade the child's work.

Practicing new vocabulary

Each unit opens with an illustrated scene that matches the course book, but with the words removed and placed in a panel. The parent or teacher should supervise the child as they listen to the accompanying audio on the website or the app and write the correct words in the spaces.

1 First, click on the corresponding unit number (here, **Unit 15**) on your screen. Then, click on the exercise number and play each audio file in turn.

2 All the words needed to complete the scene are given in a word pool.

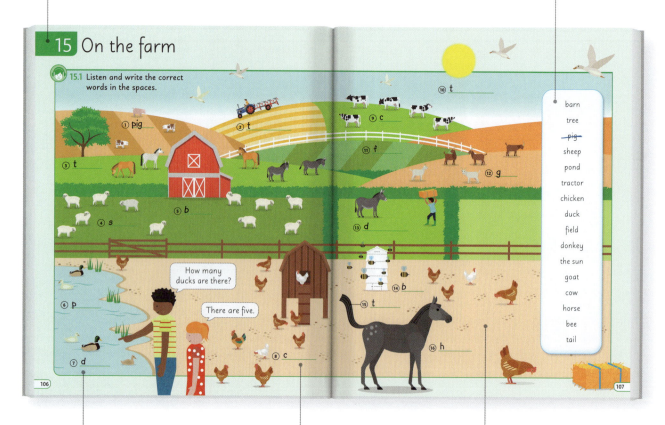

3 After listening to each word, the child should write it down in the correct space, using the panel to help them.

4 After completing the scene by writing in all the words, press **Play all** to listen to all the words again.

5 The audio pauses for a few seconds after each word. The child should repeat the word during this pause.

Practicing new grammar

Grammar is practiced in the same order that it is taught in the corresponding course book unit. Throughout the grammar exercises, vocabulary from the unit is repeated and recycled to help the child memorize it and see it used in context.

1 After revising vocabulary, the child then practices the grammar from the corresponding course book unit in exercises that reuse the unit's vocabulary.

2 Use the exercise number (here, **15.9**) to find the answers for each exercise at the back of the book, starting on page 199.

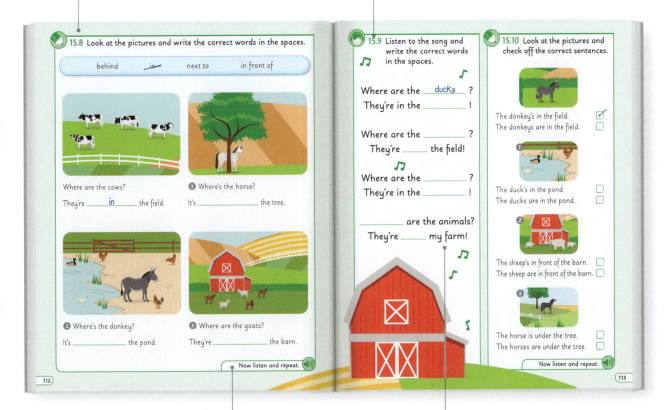

3 Most exercises have an audio recording so the child can listen to the questions and correct answers after completing each exercise.

4 All the songs from the course book are repeated, but with some words removed. The child should listen to the song and write the correct words in the spaces.

9

1.2 Listen and write the correct words in the spaces.

> I'm　　Maria　　~~Hello~~　　Max　　Hello　　name's

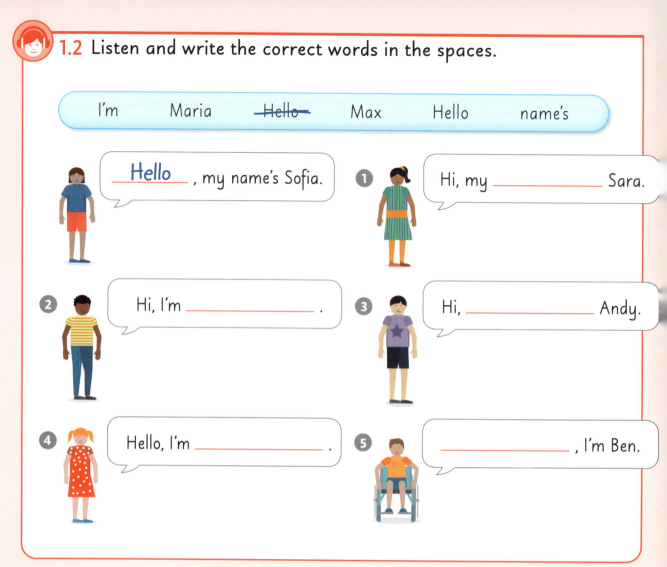

Hello, my name's Sofia.

1. Hi, my _____ Sara.

2. Hi, I'm _____ .

3. Hi, _____ Andy.

4. Hello, I'm _____ .

5. _____ , I'm Ben.

1.3 Find Max and Sara in the picture.

1.4 Listen and circle the correct names.

Ben / Maria

Andy / Sofia

Maria / Sara

Andy / Max

Maria / Sofia

Ben / Sofia

1.5 Match the numbers to the correct words.

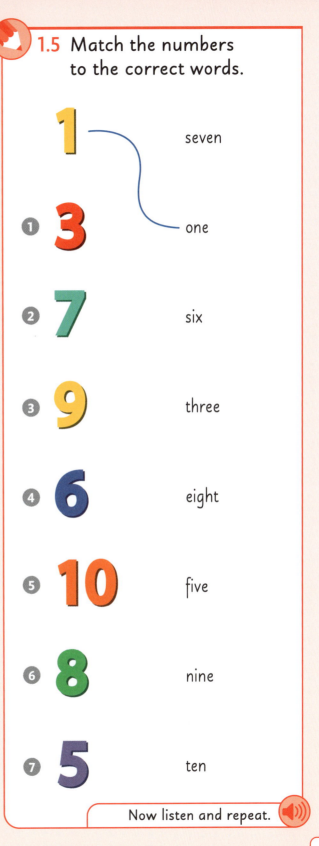

1 — seven
3 — one
7 — six
9 — three
6 — eight
10 — five
8 — nine
5 — ten

Now listen and repeat.

1.6 Listen and color in the numbers you hear.

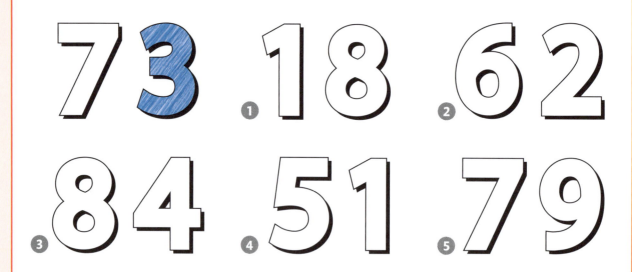

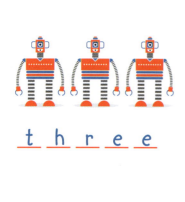 **1.7** Count and write the correct numbers under the pictures.

t h r e e

① _ _ _ _ _

② _ _ _ _

③ _ _ _ _ _

④ _ _ _ _ _

⑤ _ _ _ _

Now listen and repeat.

7. a_____
8. t_____
9. c_____
10. b_____

letters
teacher
classmate
~~playground~~
numbers
board
tablet
book
alphabet
cupboard

2.2 Look at the pictures and check off the correct words.

numbers ☐
book ☑

1 tablet ☐
board ☐

2 teacher ☐
letters ☐

3 cupboard ☐
alphabet ☐

4 board ☐
classmate ☐

5 playground ☐
book ☐

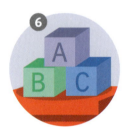

6 numbers ☐
letters ☐

7 numbers ☐
cupboard ☐

8 board ☐
classmate ☐

9 tablet ☐
cupboard ☐

Now listen and repeat.

2.3 Look at the pictures and write the words in the correct place on the crossword.

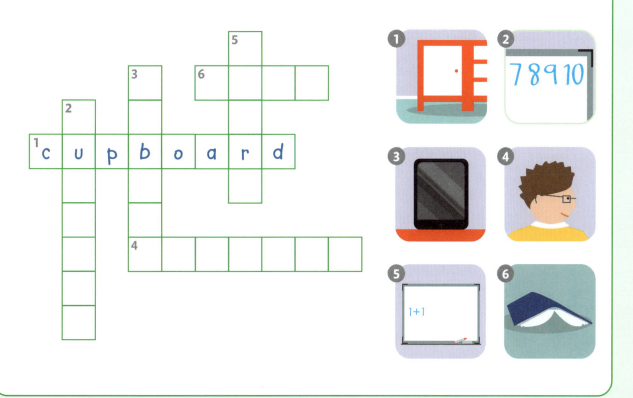

2.4 Listen and check off the correct pictures.

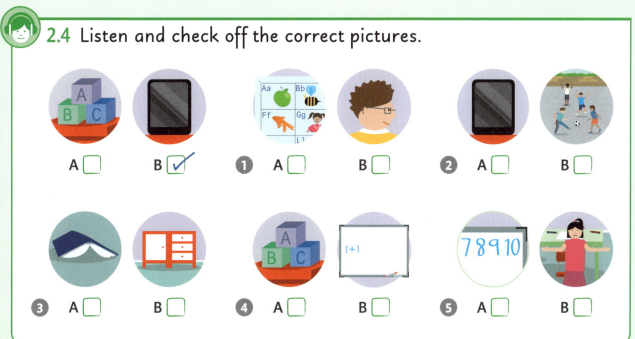

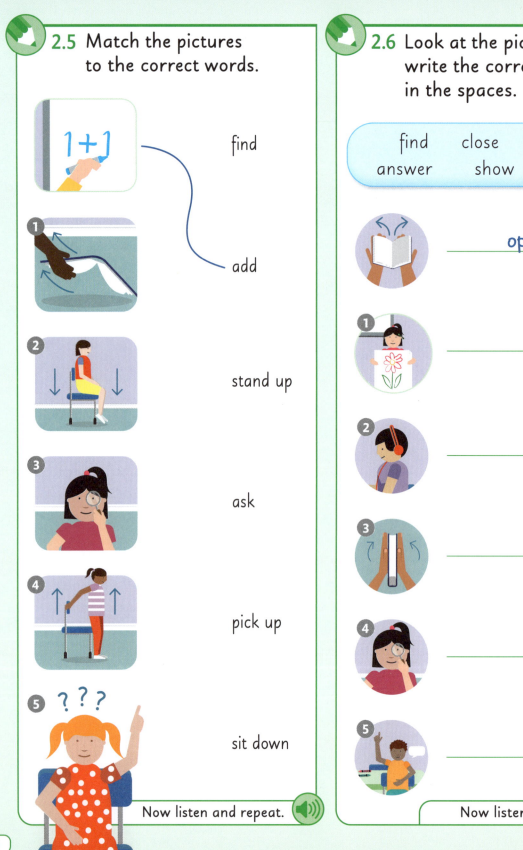

2.7 Look at the pictures and write the letters in the correct order.

l s t i n e   f d n i   a k s

l i s t e n   ① f _ _ _ _   ② a _ _

s o w h   l k o o   o n p e

③ s _ _ _ _   ④ l _ _ _   ⑤ o _ _ _ _

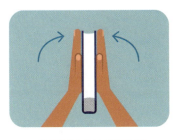

c s o l e   d d a   a r w e s n

⑥ c _ _ _ _   ⑦ a _ _   ⑧ a _ _ _ _ _

Now listen and repeat.

2.8 Look at the pictures and circle the correct words.

His / (Her) name's Sara.

❶ His / Her name's Andy.

❷ His / Her name's Ben.

❸ His / Her name's Maria.

❹ His / Her name's Max.

❺ His / Her name's Sofia.

Now listen and repeat.

2.9 Listen and match the questions to the correct answers.

What's his name? — Her name's Bella.

1 What's his name? — His name's Tom.

2 What's her name? — Her name's Amy.

3 What's his name? — His name's Ted.

4 What's her name? — His name's Dan.

5 What's her name? — Her name's Anna.

2.10 There are four sentences. Mark the beginning and end of each one and write them below.

What's her name?

1 _____

2 _____

3 _____

What'shername?|Hername'sEvie.What'shisname?Hisname'sJack.

Now listen and repeat.

3 Our classroom

3.1 Listen and write the correct words in the spaces.

3.2 Look at the pictures and circle the correct words.

draw / (count)

read / play

play / spell

draw / write

paint / count

Now listen and repeat.

3.3 Listen and check off the correct pictures.

A ☐ B ✓

① A ☐ B ☐

② A ☐ B ☐

③ A ☐ B ☐

④ A ☐ B ☐

⑤ A ☐ B ☐

3.4 Match the pictures to the correct sentences.

- Let's count!
- Let's draw!
- Let's read!
- Let's write!
- Let's play!
- Let's paint!

Now listen and repeat.

3.5 Listen to the song and write the correct words in the spaces.

Hello, __hello__ !
What's your _____ ?
How are you?
Let's _____ a game.

_____ say hello
to my new friends
_____ and Maria,
Sara and _____ .

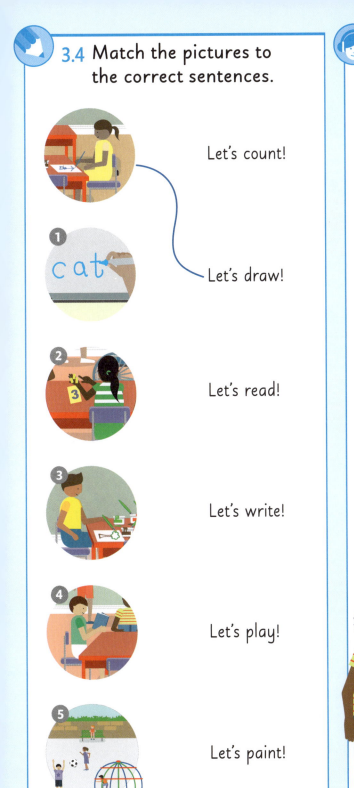

3.6 Match the numbers to the correct words.

17   **.12**   **.16**   **.15**   **.20**
　　　　①　　　　②　　　　③　　　　④

sixteen　　　　　　　twenty　　　　　　　fifteen

　　　seventeen　　　　　　twelve

Now listen and repeat.

3.7 Write the correct words under the numbers.

eighteen   ~~twelve~~   eleven   fourteen
twenty   thirteen   nineteen   sixteen   fifteen

12　　　　**.14**　　　　**.19**
　　　　　　　①　　　　　　　②
twelve　　　　_____　　　_____

.18　　　　**.11**　　　　**.16**
③　　　　　　④　　　　　　⑤
_____　　_____　　_____

.20　　　　**.13**　　　　**.15**
⑥　　　　　　⑦　　　　　　⑧
_____　　_____　　_____

Now listen and repeat.

28

3.8 Look at the pictures and circle the correct words.

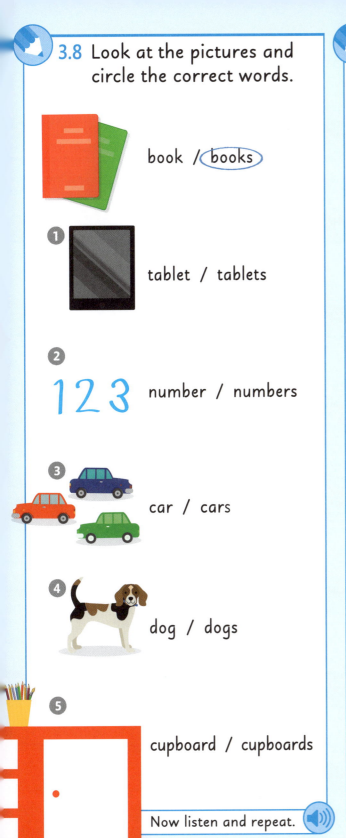

book / (books)
1. tablet / tablets
2. number / numbers
3. car / cars
4. dog / dogs
5. cupboard / cupboards

Now listen and repeat.

3.9 Read the words and check off the correct pictures.

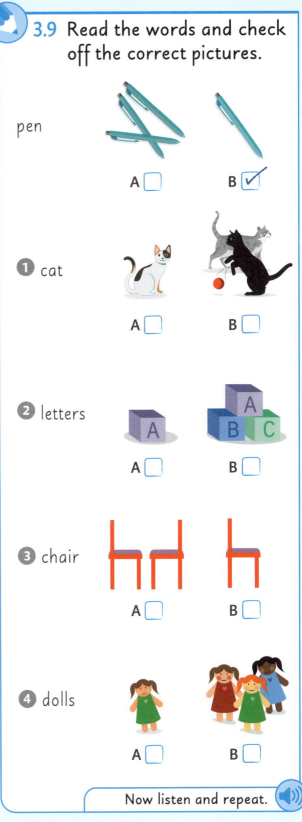

pen — A ☐ B ✓
1. cat — A ☐ B ☐
2. letters — A ☐ B ☐
3. chair — A ☐ B ☐
4. dolls — A ☐ B ☐

Now listen and repeat.

4 My things

4.1 Listen and write the correct words in the spaces.

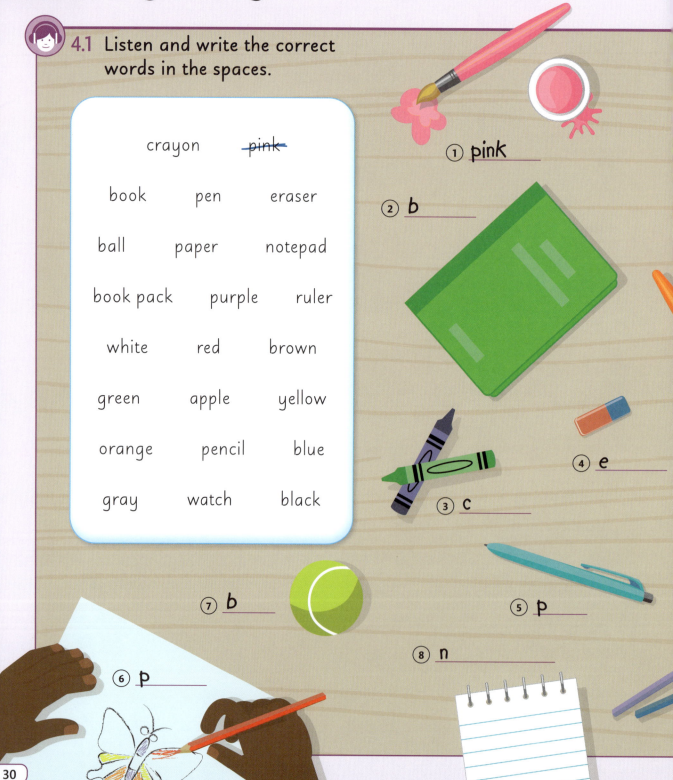

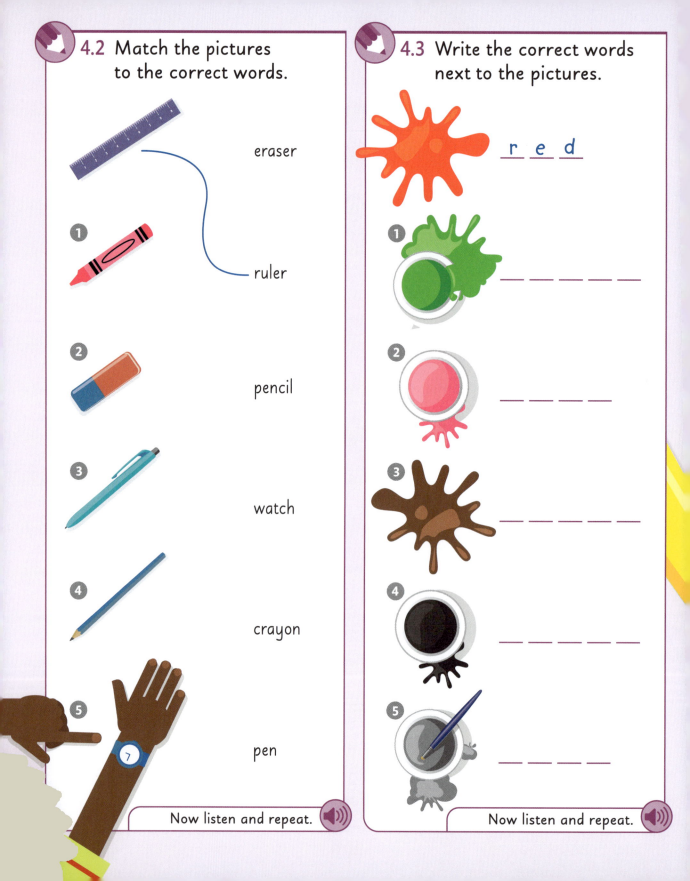

4.4 Look at the pictures and check off the correct words.

white ☐
blue ☑
pink ☐

1
purple ☐
green ☐
crayon ☐

2
watch ☐
ruler ☐
book pack ☐

3
paper ☐
white ☐
watch ☐

4
pink ☐
notepad ☐
red ☐

5
orange ☐
blue ☐
apple ☐

6
red ☐
crayon ☐
yellow ☐

7
paper ☐
brown ☐
pencil ☐

Now listen and repeat.

4.5 Listen and check off the correct pictures.

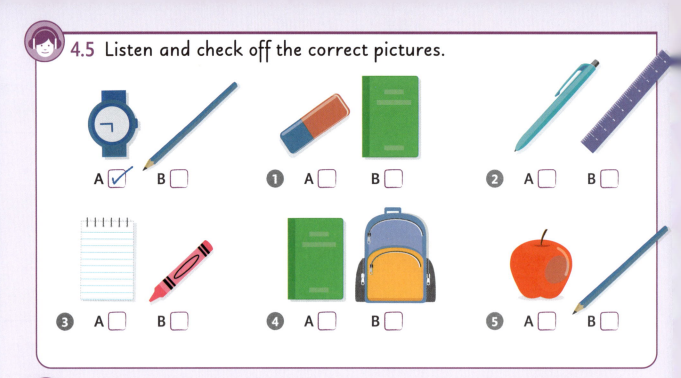

4.6 Look at the pictures and write the correct answers in the spaces.

It's a ball.   ~~They're books.~~
It's a watch.   They're rulers.

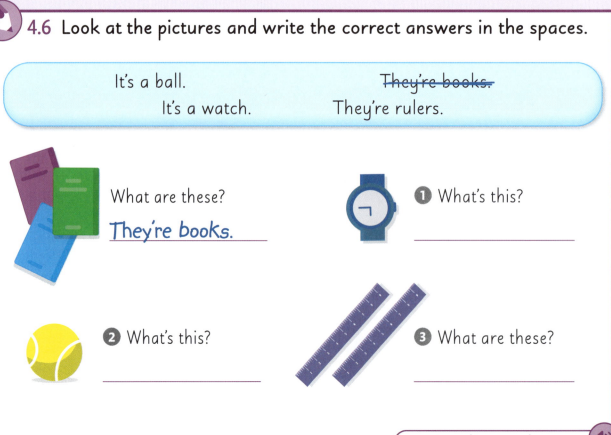

What are these?
They're books.

1 What's this?

2 What's this?

3 What are these?

Now listen and repeat.

4.7 Look at the pictures and write the correct words in the spaces.

It's   What are   They're   ~~What's~~   these   apple

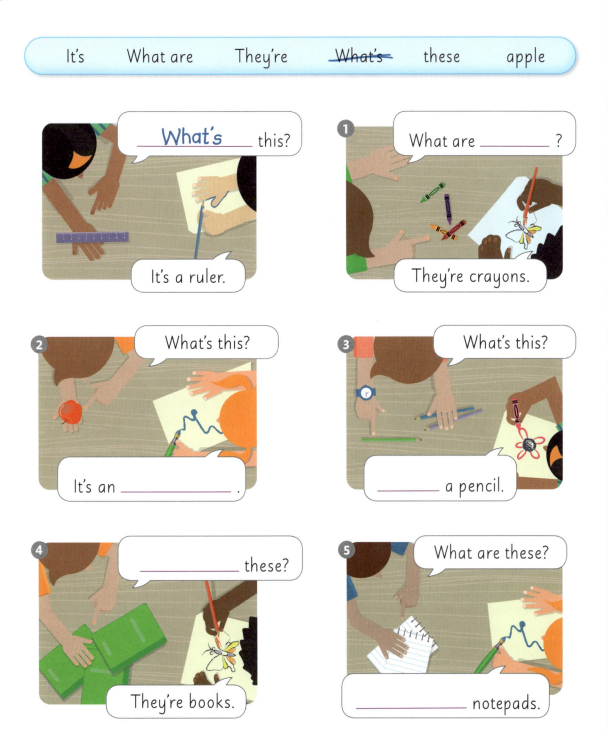

Now listen and repeat.

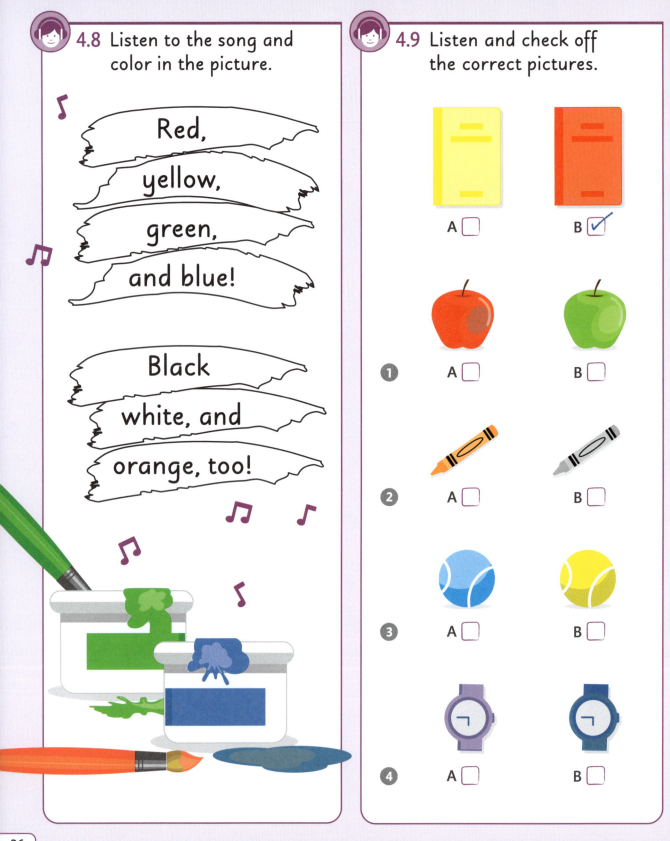

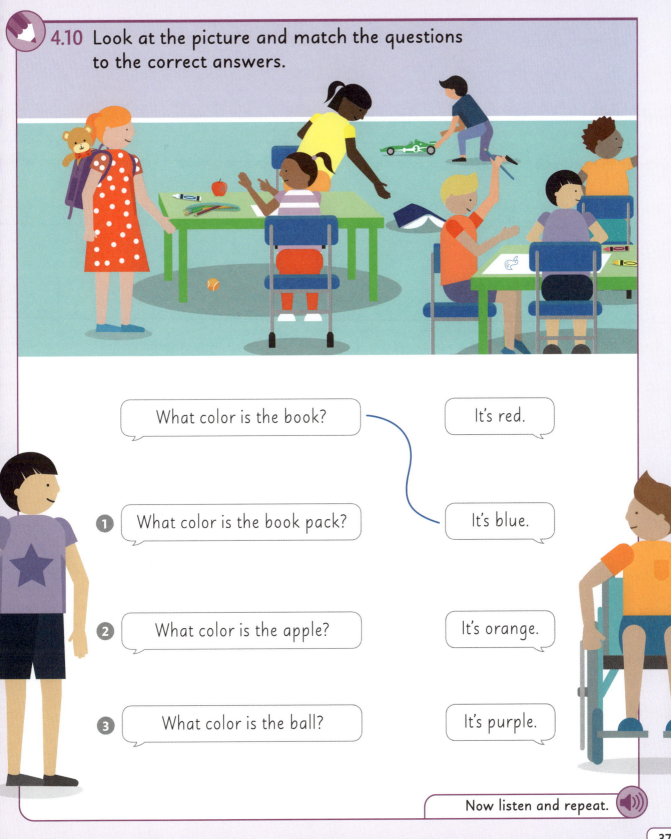

5 Our favorite animals

5.1 Listen and write the correct words in the spaces.

5.2 Look at the pictures and circle the correct words.

giraffe / (frog)   ❶ hippo / polar bear   ❷ lion / parrot

❸ tiger / snake   ❹ bear / elephant   ❺ crocodile / bird

Now listen and repeat.

5.3 Find and circle the five words in the grid.

bear
lizard
~~snake~~
whale
frog
bird

w s f r o g
h g a s l v
a b w n z x
l i z a r d
e r y k c k
f d b e a r

40

5.4 Look at the pictures and write the letters in the correct order.

s a k n e

s n a k e

1

w l h a e

w _ _ _ _

2

l o n i

l _ _ _

3

z b a e r

z _ _ _ _

4

b r a e

b _ _ _

Now listen and repeat.

5.5 Listen to the song and write the correct words in the spaces.

Animals, animals everywhere!
A ___lion___ , a giraffe, and a _____ .

A _____ and
a _____ ,
a tiger and a _____ ,
animals, animals,
they are great!

5.6 Look at the pictures and write the correct words in the spaces.

What's   that   They're   ~~frog~~

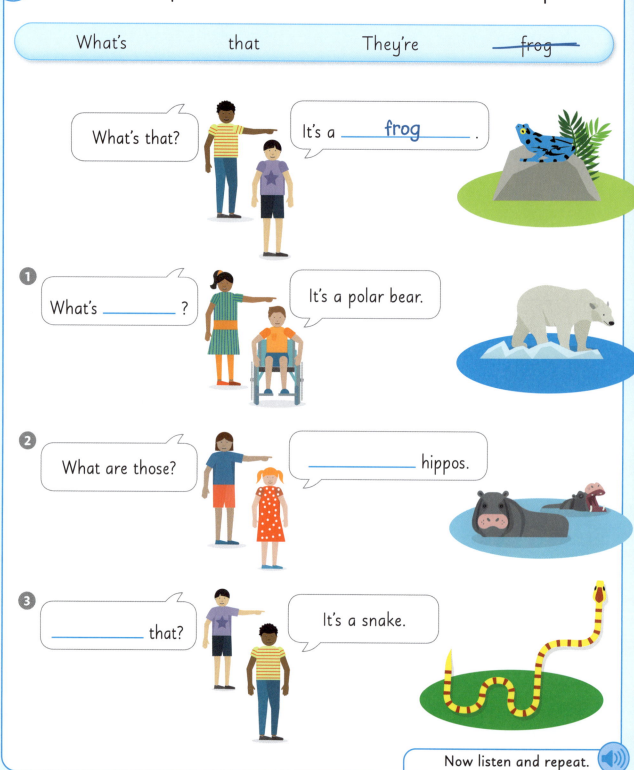

5.7 Look at the pictures and write the correct answers in the spaces.

It's a crocodile. ~~They're monkeys.~~
They're parrots.   It's a zebra.

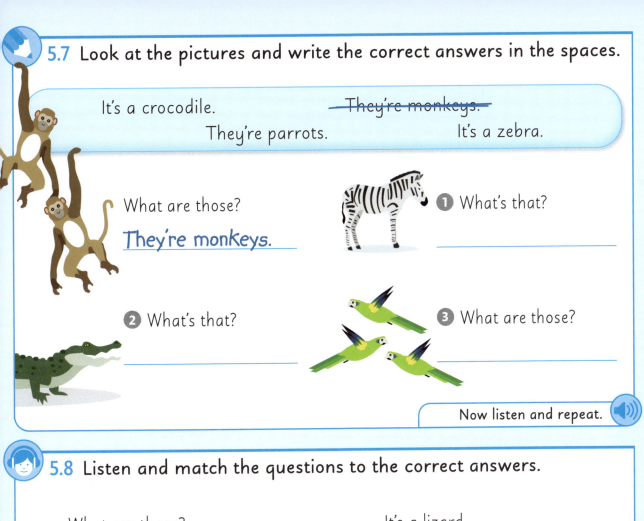

What are those?
They're monkeys.

❶ What's that?

❷ What's that?

❸ What are those?

Now listen and repeat.

5.8 Listen and match the questions to the correct answers.

What are those? — It's a lizard.
❶ What's that?   It's a bird.
❷ What are those?   They're elephants.
❸ What's that? —— They're lions.
❹ What are those?   It's a parrot.
❺ What's that?   They're penguins.

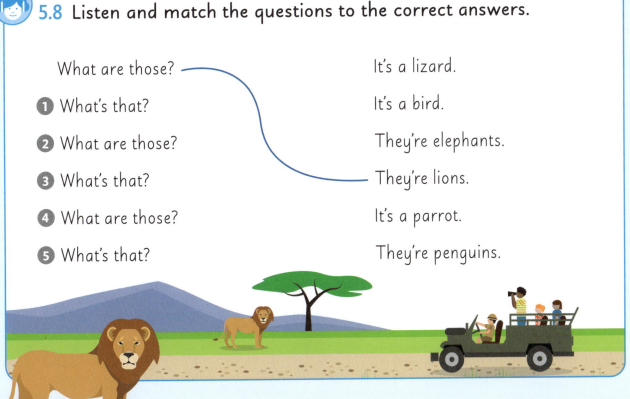

43

5.9 There are four sentences. Mark the beginning and end of each one and write them below.

Whatarethose?|They'retigers.What'sthat?It'sanelephant.

What are those?

1 _____

2 _____

3 _____

Now listen and repeat.

5.10 Listen and check off the correct pictures.

A ☐   B ✓

1 A ☐   B ☐

2 A ☐   B ☐

3 A ☐   B ☐

4 A ☐   B ☐

5 A ☐   B ☐

5.11 Look at the pictures and write the correct words in the spaces.

> bird   ~~frog~~   monkey   bear   elephant   lizard

 What's your favorite animal? My favorite animal is a __frog__.

1. What's your favorite animal?  My favorite animal is a _____.

2. What's your favorite animal? My favorite animal is a _____.

3. What's your favorite animal? My favorite animal is a _____.

4. What's your favorite animal? My favorite animal is an _____.

5. What's your favorite animal? My favorite animal is a _____.

Now listen and repeat.

6 This is my family

6.1 Listen and write the correct words in the spaces.

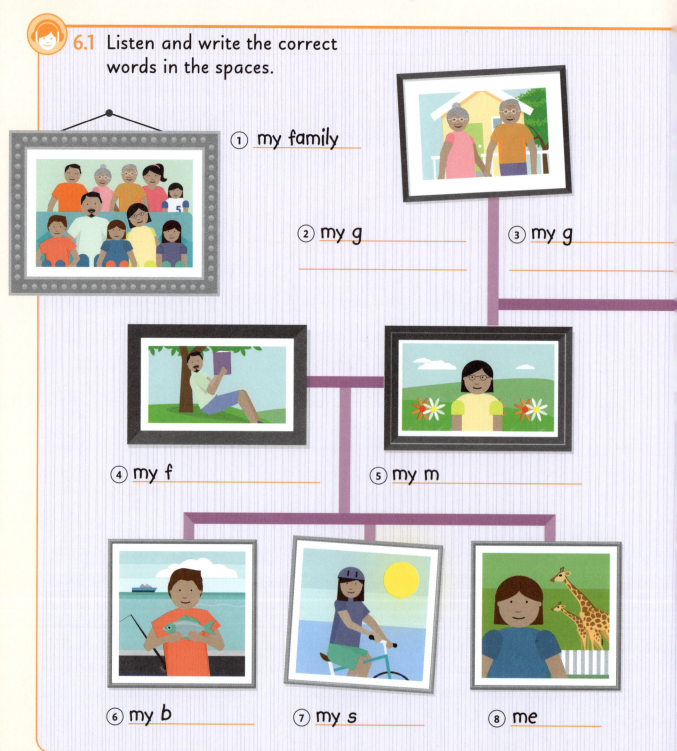

1. my family
2. my g
3. my g
4. my f
5. my m
6. my b
7. my s
8. me

~~my family~~ my mother/mom ~~me~~
my grandmother/grandma my brother my aunt
my father/dad my sister my uncle
my cousin my grandfather/grandpa

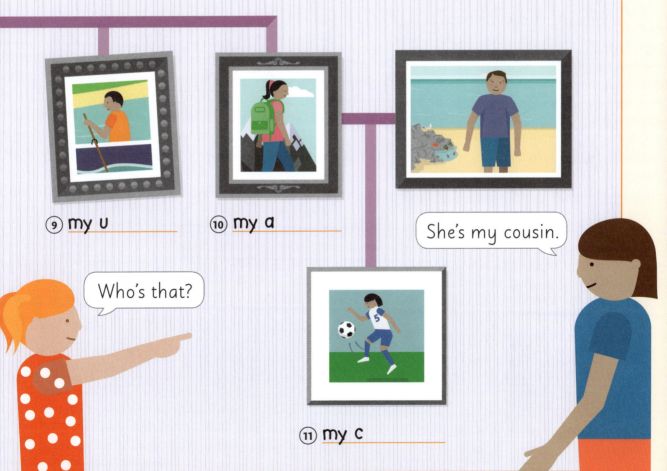

9. my u_____
10. my a_____
11. my c_____

Who's that?

She's my cousin.

6.4 Look at the pictures and write the correct words in the spaces.

grandma   ~~brother~~   uncle   cousin   sister   dad

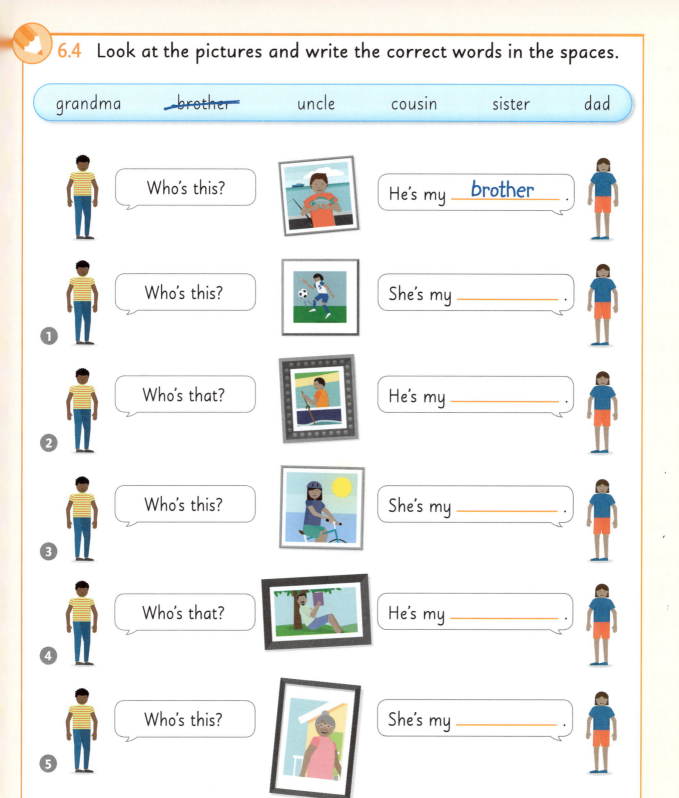

1. Who's this? — He's my _brother_.
   Who's this? — She's my _____.
2. Who's that? — He's my _____.
3. Who's this? — She's my _____.
4. Who's that? — He's my _____.
5. Who's this? — She's my _____.

Now listen and repeat.

6.5 Listen and check off the correct answers.

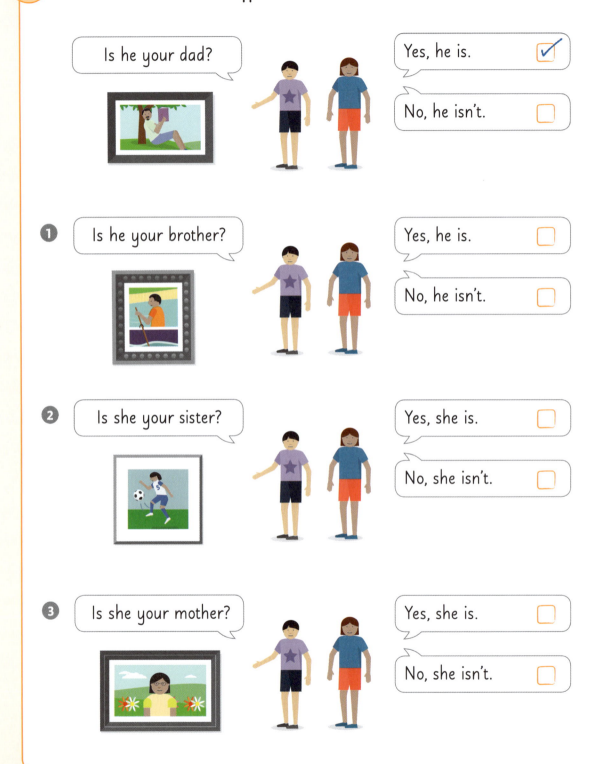

6.6 Match the pictures to the correct words.

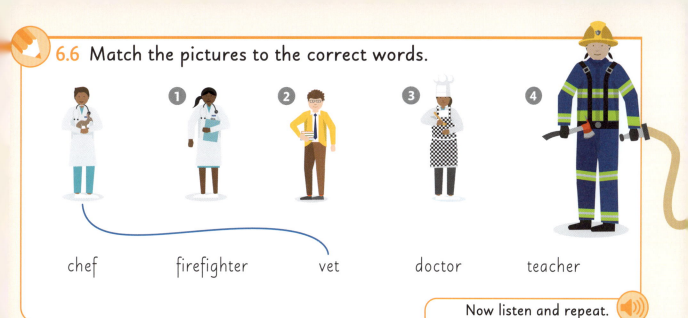

chef   firefighter   vet   doctor   teacher

Now listen and repeat.

6.7 Find and circle the four words in the grid.

teacher   vet   ~~doctor~~   farmer   chef

```
d o c t o r g f
t v y i j w r a
t e a c h e r r
f t r h y f h m
a q g l m b q e
w c h e f d m r
```

6.8 Look at the pictures and write the correct words in the spaces.

> teacher   ~~farmer~~   chef
> doctor   police officer

He's a ____farmer____ .

① She's a _____ .

② He's a _____ .

③ She's a _____ .

④ She's a _____ .

Now listen and repeat.

6.9 Look at the pictures and check off the correct sentences.

He's a firefighter. ✔
She's a firefighter. ☐

1. He's a doctor. ☐
She's a doctor. ☐

2. She's a chef. ☐
He's a chef. ☐

3. He's a farmer. ☐
She's a farmer. ☐

4. He's a teacher. ☐
She's a teacher. ☐

5. She's a police officer. ☐
He's a police officer. ☐

Now listen and repeat. 🔊

6.10 Listen to the song and write the correct words in the spaces.

Who's this?
She's my _____mother_____ .
Who's that?
He's my _____ .

My _____ is a teacher,
my _____ is a vet,
Grandpa's a _____ ,
and Grandma's a _____ !

5

53

7 This is my room

7.1 Listen and write the correct words in the spaces.

7.2 Match the pictures to the correct words.

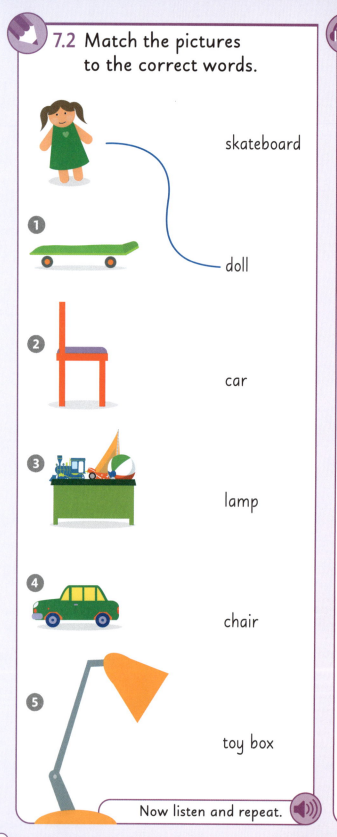

skateboard
doll
car
lamp
chair
toy box

Now listen and repeat.

7.3 Listen and check off the correct pictures.

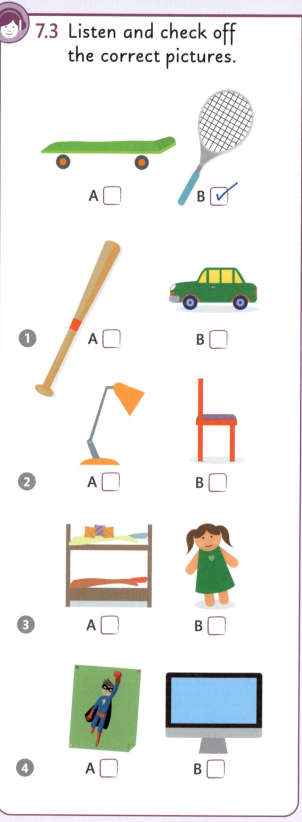

56

7.4 Read the sentences and check off the correct pictures.

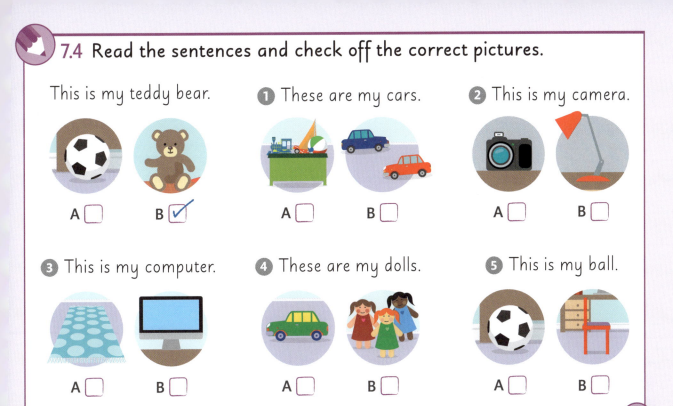

Now listen and repeat.

7.5 Listen and match the names to the correct pictures.

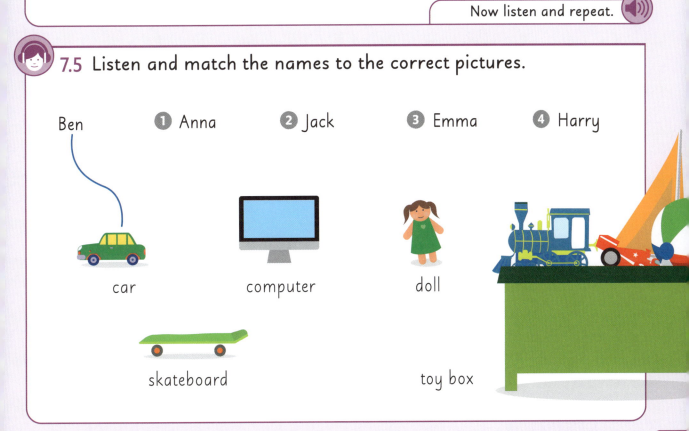

7.6 Look at the pictures and write the correct words in the spaces.

> Those are   That's   ~~This is~~   That's
> This is   These are

__This is__ my doll.

❶ _____ my ball.

❷ _____ my cameras.

❸ _____ my teddy bears.

❹ _____ my toy box.

❺ _____ my tennis racket.

Now listen and repeat.

7.7 Look at the pictures and write the correct names in the spaces.

Maria

Andy

I have a computer.

Maria

① I have a rug.

_____

② I don't have a doll.

_____

③ I don't have a chair.

_____

④ I have a skateboard.

_____

⑤ I don't have a lamp.

_____

⑥ I have a teddy bear.

_____

⑦ I don't have a car.

_____

Now listen and repeat.

7.8 Listen and write the correct answers below.

> Yes, I do.   ~~No, I don't.~~   No, I don't.
> No, I don't.   Yes, I do.

Do you have a baseball bat?

No, I don't.

1 Do you have a car?

2 Do you have a chair?

3 Do you have a lamp?

4 Do you have a desk?

7.9 Look at the pictures and check off the correct answers.

Do you have a car?
Yes, I do. ☐
No, I don't. ☑

1 Do you have a rug?
Yes, I do. ☐
No, I don't. ☐

2 Do you have a ball?
Yes, I do. ☐
No, I don't. ☐

3 Do you have a poster?
Yes, I do. ☐
No, I don't. ☐

4 Do you have a doll?
Yes, I do. ☐
No, I don't. ☐

5 Do you have a desk?
Yes, I do. ☐
No, I don't. ☐

Now listen and repeat. 🔊

7.10 Listen to the song and write the correct words in the spaces.

This is my _____toy box_____
and these are my _____ ,
I have a _____
and a _____ , too.
Toys are fantastic!
Toys are cool!

61

8 Review: This is me

 8.1 Listen and read.

My name's Max.
I'm ten years old.
My favorite animal is a hippo.
I have a tablet.
I don't have a computer.

My favorite toy is my ball.

8.2 Write about yourself then draw your room and your favorite toy.

My name's _____ .
I'm _____ years old.
My favorite animal is _____ .
I have a _____ .
I don't have a _____ .

My favorite toy is my _____ .

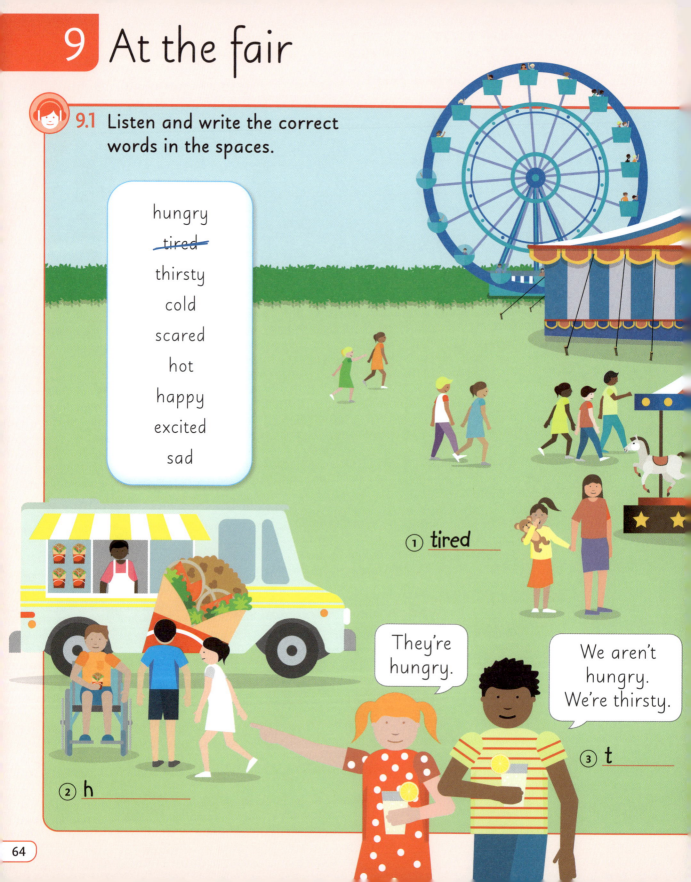

④ s _____
⑤ h _____ ⑥ c _____
⑦ e _____
⑧ s _____ ⑨ h _____

9.2 Look at the pictures and circle the correct words.

excited / tired   cold / hungry   scared / excited

thirsty / hungry   sad / tired   happy / hot

Now listen and repeat.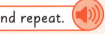

9.3 Listen and check off the correct pictures.

A ☐   B ✓   ① A ☐   B ☐   ② A ☐   B ☐

③ A ☐   B ☐   ④ A ☐   B ☐   ⑤ A ☐   B ☐

9.4 Look at the pictures and write the correct words next to the pictures.

> happy ~~cold~~ tired
> excited thirsty

cold

1. _____

2. _____

3. _____

4. _____

Now listen and repeat.

9.5 Listen to the song and write the correct words in the spaces.

Are you __happy__ ?
_____ , we are!
We are at the fair.

Are you _____ ?
_____ , we aren't.
We aren't tired
or _____ !

9.8 Look at the pictures and write the correct words in the spaces.

hot   ~~thirsty~~   really   happy   excited

They're very _thirsty_ .

1 We're really _____ .

2 They're _____ .

3 We're _____ .

4 We're _____ tired.

Now listen and repeat.

9.9 Look at the pictures and check off the correct answers.

 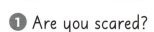 

Are they excited?
Yes, they are. ☐
No, they're not. ☑

① Are you scared?
Yes, we are. ☐
No, we're not. ☐

② Are you hot?
Yes, we are. ☐
No, we're not. ☐

③ Are they cold?
Yes, they are. ☐
No, they're not. ☐

④ Are you tired?
Yes, we are. ☐
No, we're not. ☐

⑤ Are they sad?
Yes, they are. ☐
No, they're not. ☐

Now listen and repeat.

9.10 Listen and match the questions to the correct answers.

Are you sad?   Yes, they are.

① Are they happy?   No, we're not.

② Are you excited?   No, they're not.

③ Are you hungry?   No, we're not.

④ Are they scared?   Yes, we are.

9.11 Look at the pictures and write the correct answers in the spaces.

> No, we're not.   Yes, they are.   ~~Yes, we are.~~   No, they're not.
> Yes, they are.   No, we're not.   No, they're not.   Yes, we are.

Are you cold?
Yes, we are.

❶ Are they hungry?

❷ Are you happy?

❸ Are they thirsty?

❹ Are they excited?

❺ Are you scared?

❻ Are you excited?

❼ Are they happy?

Now listen and repeat.

71

10 Our pets

10.1 Listen and write the correct words in the spaces.

10.4 Look at the pictures and write the correct words.

vet   ~~fish~~   dog   mouse   tortoise   cat

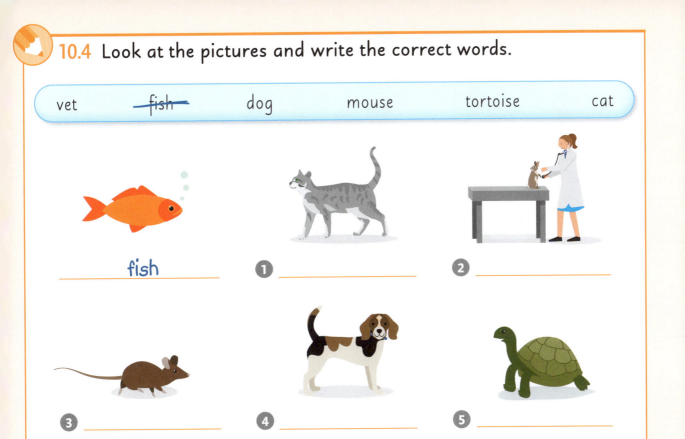

Now listen and repeat.

10.5 Listen and check off the correct pictures.

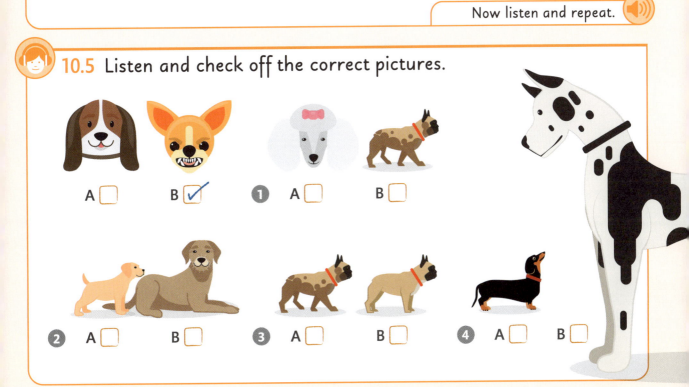

10.6 Listen to the song and write the correct words in the spaces.

I have a ___cat___ ,
she's _____ and _____ .
She likes to run
and play with a ball.

Maria has a _____ ,
his name is Socks.
He's _____ and _____
and he's in this box.

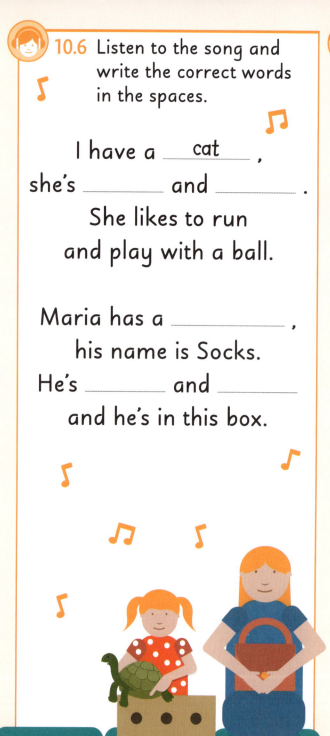

10.7 Match the pictures to the correct words.

Ben has a rabbit.

1

He has a mouse.

2

She has a fish.

3

Sara has a tortoise.

4

He has a cat.

5

She has a cat.

Now listen and repeat.

10.9 Look at the pictures and check off the correct answers.

Does she have a dog? Yes, she does. ☐
No, she doesn't. ✓

① Does he have a cat? Yes, he does. ☐
No, he doesn't. ☐

② Does she have a tortoise? Yes, she does. ☐
No, she doesn't. ☐

③ Does he have a spider? Yes, he does. ☐
No, he doesn't. ☐

Now listen and repeat.

10.10 Read the questions and check off the correct pictures.

Which dog is clean?

A ☑   B ☐

1 Which one is nice?

A ☐   B ☐

2 Which dog is small?

A ☐   B ☐

3 Which one is young?

A ☐   B ☐

4 Which dog is dirty?

A ☐   B ☐

5 Which one is old?

A ☐   B ☐

Now listen and repeat.

10.11 There are four sentences. Mark the beginning and end of each one and write them below.

Which pet is small?

1 _____

2 _____

3 _____

Whichpetissmall? Themouse.Whichoneisscary?Thespider!

Now listen and repeat.

11 My body

11.1 Listen and write the correct words in the spaces.

body   nose   mouth   face   ~~hair~~   arm   hand   toes   long hair   foot   leg   feet   fingers   head   ear   short hair   teeth   eye

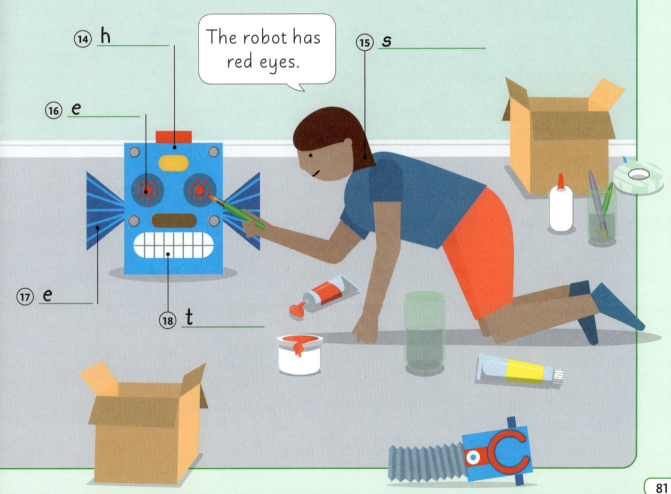

⑭ h _____
⑮ s _____
⑯ e _____
⑰ e _____
⑱ t _____

The robot has red eyes.

11.2 Find and circle the five words in the grid.

teeth   fingers   ~~leg~~   hair   feet   arm

```
d  g  f  l  b  x  a
t  e  e  t  h  h  r
r (l  e  g) n  a  m
j  k  t  k  b  i  f
f  i  n  g  e  r  s
```

11.3 Match the pictures to the correct words.

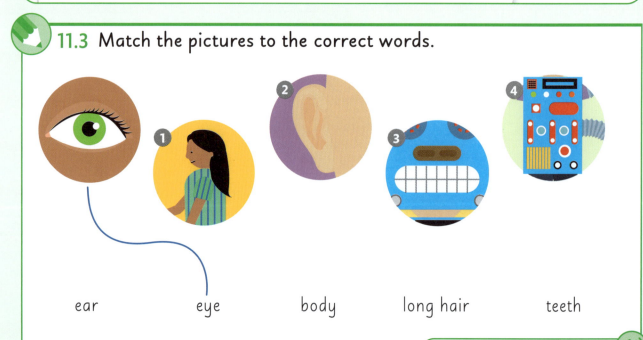

ear   eye   body   long hair   teeth

Now listen and repeat.

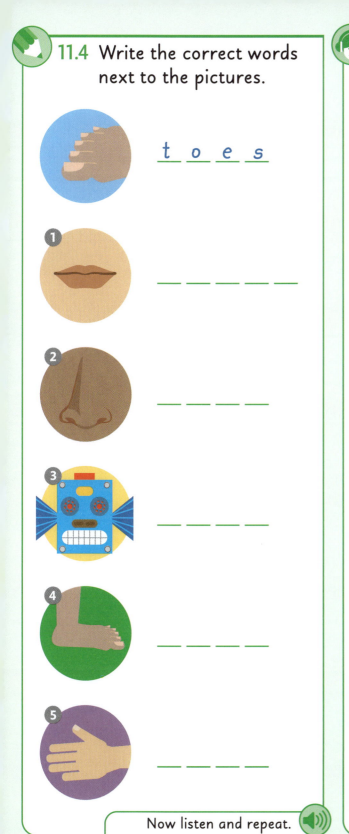
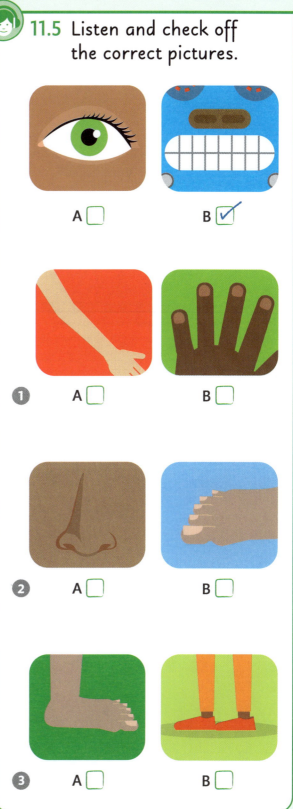

11.6 Look at the picture and write the correct words in the spaces.

legs   purple   ~~ears~~   teeth
hands   yellow   blue

The robot has green ___ears___ .

1. The robot has _____ eyes.

2. It has red _____ .

3. It has purple _____ .

4. The robot has _____ feet.

5. It has a _____ nose.

6. The robot has orange _____ .

Now listen and repeat.

11.7 Listen and color in the robot.

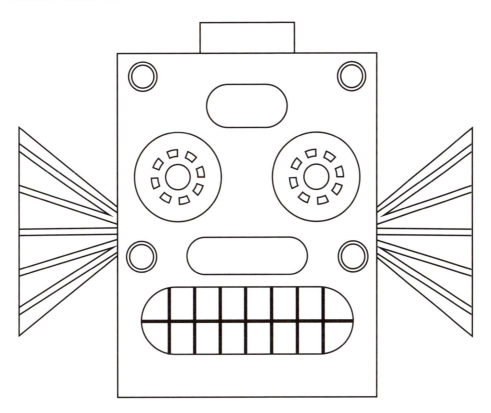

11.8 Listen and circle the correct answers.

Does the robot have four arms?
(Yes, it does) / No, it doesn't.

❶ Does it have black feet?
Yes, it does. / No, it doesn't.

❷ Does it have green eyes?
Yes, it does. / No, it doesn't.

❸ Does the robot have orange teeth?
Yes, it does. / No, it doesn't.

❹ Does the robot have two legs?
Yes, it does. / No, it doesn't.

❺ Does it have purple toes?
Yes, it does. / No, it doesn't.

85

11.9 Look at the picture and write the correct answers in the spaces.

> No, it doesn't.   ~~Yes, it does.~~   Yes, it does.
> Yes, it does.   No, it doesn't.   Yes, it does.

Does it have three arms?

Yes, it does.

❶ Does it have purple eyes?

_____

❷ Does it have two legs?

_____

❸ Does it have orange hands?

_____

❹ Does it have blue ears?

_____

❺ Does it have three hands?

_____

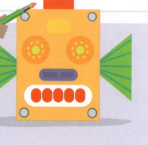

Now listen and repeat.

11.10 Match the pictures to the correct words.

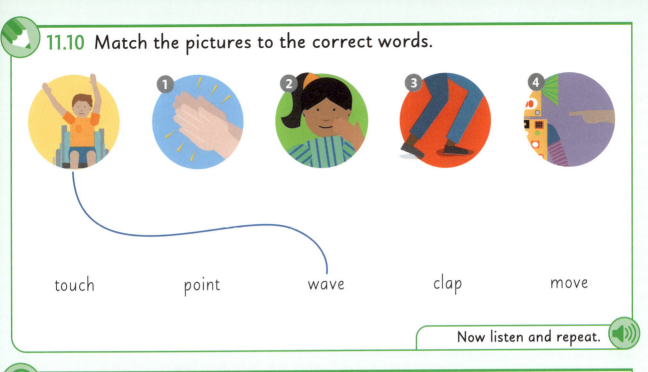

touch   point   wave   clap   move

Now listen and repeat.

11.11 Listen to the song and write the correct words in the spaces.

<u> Clap </u> your hands,
_____ your nose,
_____ your feet,
_____ your toes!

Point one _____,
move your head,
_____ your arms,
touch one leg!

12 Our town

12.1 Listen and write the correct words in the spaces.

park   airplane
train   ~~airport~~   lake
bookstore   zoo
street   boat   bike
fire station   house
school   helicopter
apartment block
store   hospital
bus   truck
motorcycle   car

① airport
② a_____
③ s_____
④ t_____
⑤ b_____
⑥ z_____
⑦ p_____
⑧ b_____

Where do you live?

I live next to the fire station.

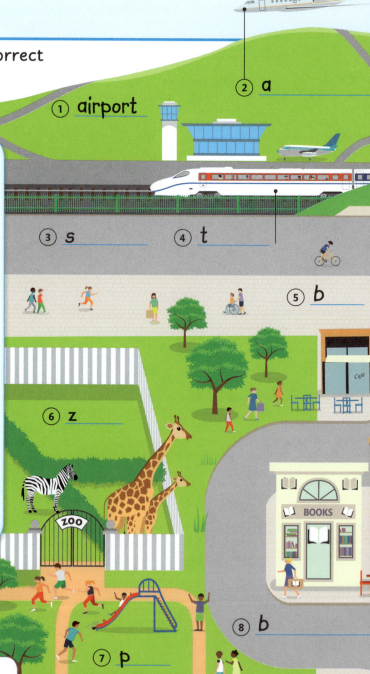

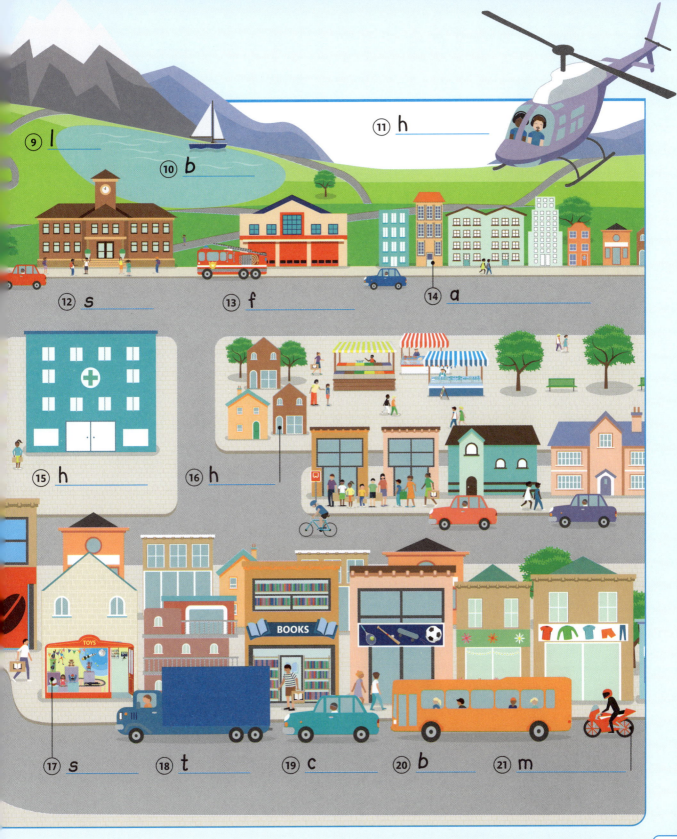

⑨ l_____ ⑩ b_____ ⑪ h_____
⑫ s_____ ⑬ f_____ ⑭ a_____
⑮ h_____ ⑯ h_____
⑰ s_____ ⑱ t_____ ⑲ c_____ ⑳ b_____ ㉑ m_____

12.2 Look at the pictures and circle the correct words.

(zoo) / street   bus / truck   house / school

bike / helicopter   hospital / store   park / truck

Now listen and repeat.

12.3 Listen and check off the correct pictures.

A ✓   B ☐   ① A ☐   B ☐   ② A ☐   B ☐

③ A ☐   B ☐   ④ A ☐   B ☐   ⑤ A ☐   B ☐

12.4 Look at the pictures and write the letters in the correct order.

h u s e o
h o u s e

c r a
c _ _ _

t a i r n
t _ _ _ _ _

l k a e
l _ _ _ _

p r k a
p _ _ _ _

Now listen and repeat.

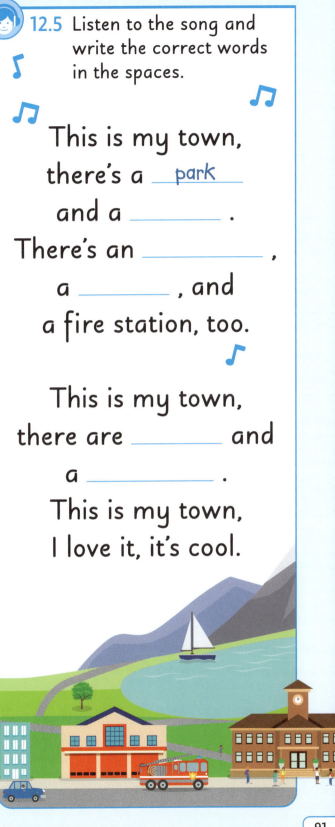

12.5 Listen to the song and write the correct words in the spaces.

This is my town,
there's a ___park___
and a _____ .
There's an _____ ,
a _____ , and
a fire station, too.

This is my town,
there are _____ and
a _____ .
This is my town,
I love it, it's cool.

91

12.6 Look at the pictures and write the correct words in the spaces.

> There are   ~~There's~~   There are   There's   There are   There's

There's a lake.

① _____ two stores.

② _____ a fire station.

③ _____ a zoo.

④ _____ three houses.

⑤ _____ four cars.

Now listen and repeat.

12.7 Read the sentences and check off the correct pictures.

There are two motorcycles.

A ☐   B ✓

① There's a car.

A ☐   B ☐

② There are four bikes.

A ☐   B ☐

③ There are three boats.

A ☐   B ☐

④ There's a house.

A ☐   B ☐

⑤ There's a truck.

A ☐   B ☐

Now listen and repeat.

12.8 Look at the pictures and check off the correct words.

behind ✓
next to ☐
in front of ☐

①

between ☐
in front of ☐
behind ☐

②

between ☐
next to ☐
in front of ☐

③

behind ☐
between ☐
next to ☐

Now listen and repeat.

93

12.9 Look at the picture and write the correct words in the spaces.

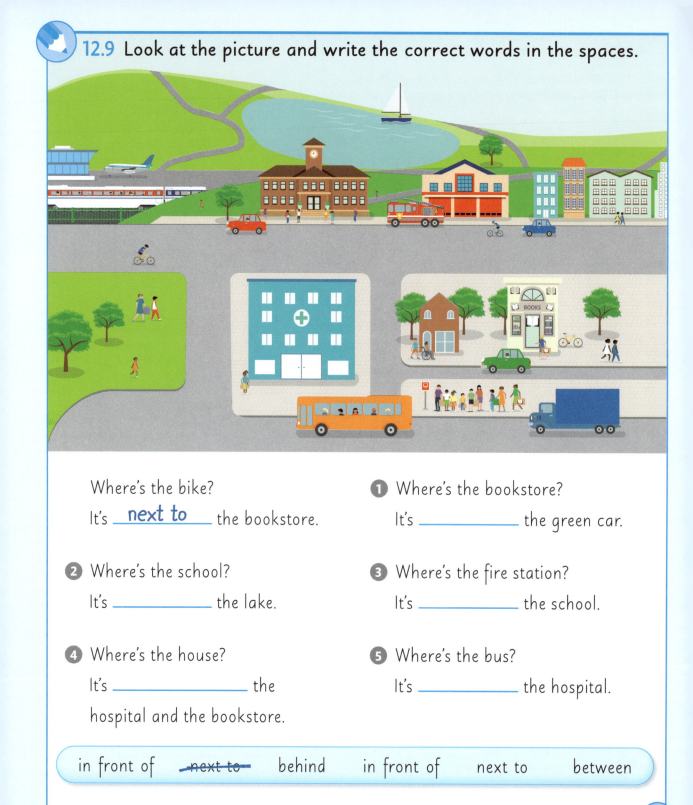

Where's the bike?
It's __next to__ the bookstore.

❶ Where's the bookstore?
It's _____ the green car.

❷ Where's the school?
It's _____ the lake.

❸ Where's the fire station?
It's _____ the school.

❹ Where's the house?
It's _____ the hospital and the bookstore.

❺ Where's the bus?
It's _____ the hospital.

in front of   ~~next to~~   behind   in front of   next to   between

Now listen and repeat.

12.10 **Listen and match the questions to the correct answers.**

Where do you live? — It's behind the hospital.

1. Where's the park? — It's between the fire station and the store.

2. Where's the truck? — It's behind the school.

3. Where's the zoo? — I live in front of the zoo.

4. Where's the lake? — It's between the airport and the apartment block.

5. Where's the school? — It's next to the lake.

I live next to the zoo.

And you?

I live _____

_____

95

13 My home

13.1 Listen and write the correct words in the spaces.

plants	bedroom
clock	~~garden~~
television/TV	
couch bath floor	
living room wall	
door window kitchen	
mat refrigerator	
armchair dining room	
bookcase hall chair	
mirror lights table	
bathroom flowers	

② b_____
③ c_____
④ p_____

⑬ l_____
⑭ t_____
⑮ c_____

① __garden__

Where's Sara?

She's in the bedroom.

96

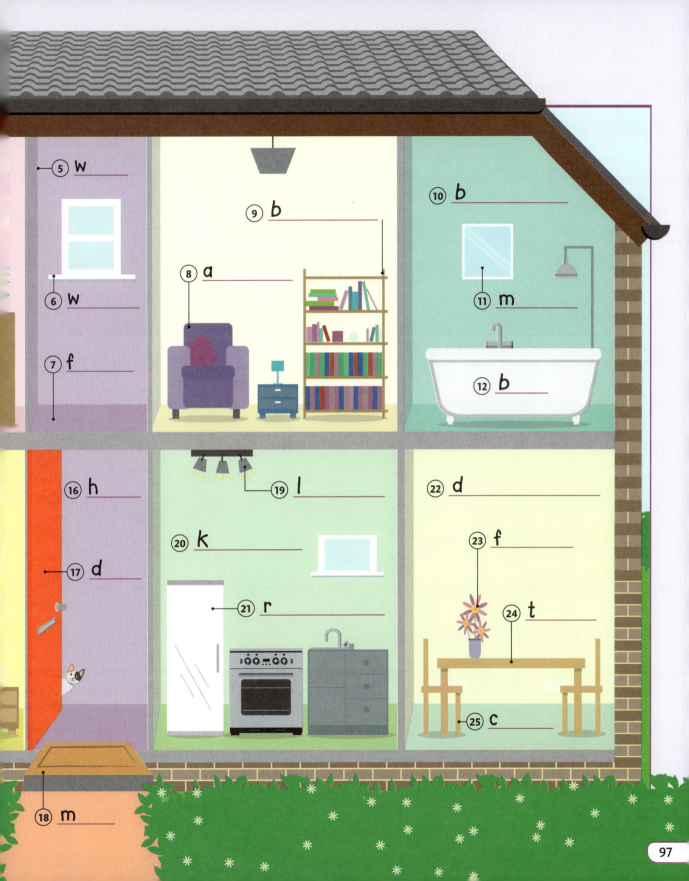

13.2 Look at the pictures and circle the correct words.

  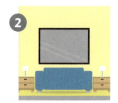

kitchen / (bathroom)   dining room / bathroom   bedroom / living room

kitchen / living room   bedroom / dining room   kitchen / hall

Now listen and repeat.

13.3 Match the pictures to the correct words.

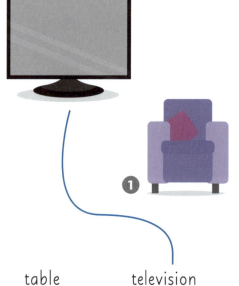 

table   television   lights   armchair   window

Now listen and repeat.

98

13.4 Look at the pictures and check off the correct words.

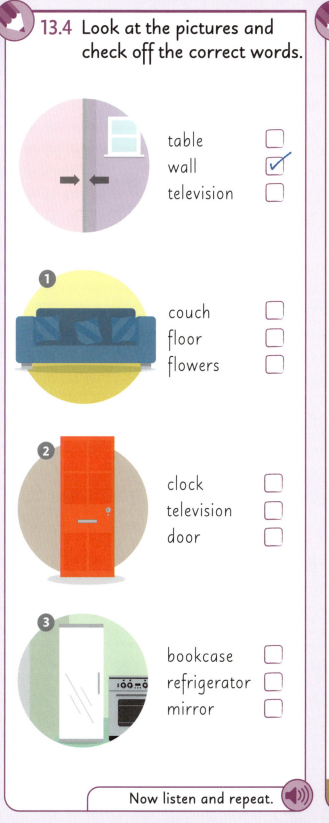

13.5 Look at the pictures and write the correct words in the spaces.

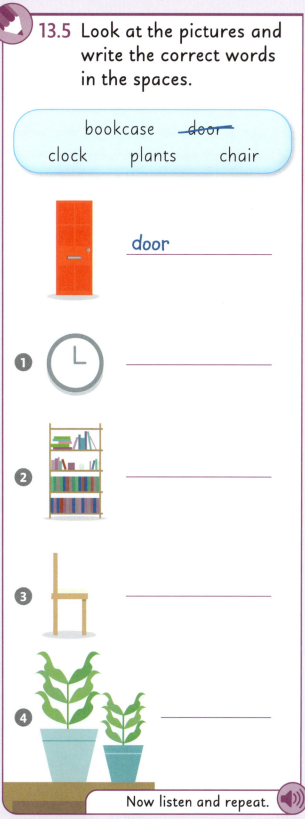

Now listen and repeat.

13.6 Write the correct words under the pictures.

under ~~in~~ on

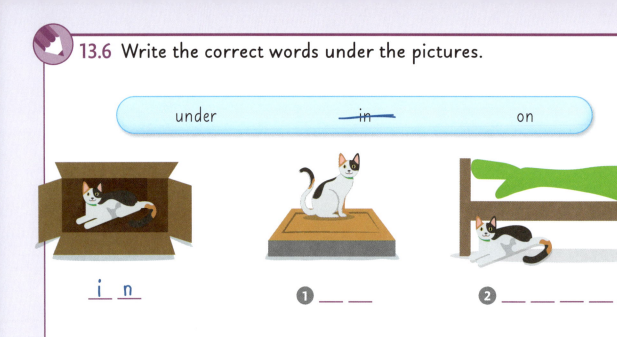

i n

1 _ _

2 _ _ _ _ _

Now listen and repeat.

13.7 Look at the pictures and circle the correct words.

The book is
(on) / **under** the floor.

The cat is
in / **on** the bath.

The plants are
on / **under** the window.

The cat is
on / **in** the mat.

The bookcase is
under / **on** the lights.

The flowers are
in / **on** the table.

Now listen and repeat.

100

13.8 Listen and check off the correct pictures.

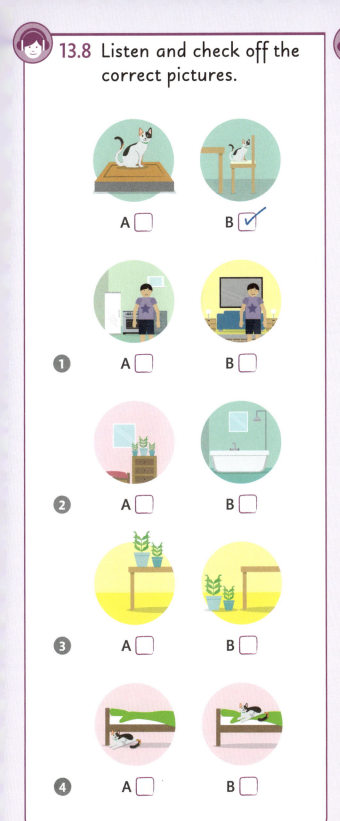

13.9 Listen to the song and write the correct words in the spaces.

The TV's __in__ the living room,
the ____ is in the ____ .

Where's the ____ ?
It's ____ my
bedroom ____ .

13.10 Look at the pictures and write the correct answers in the spaces.

> Yes, there is.   ~~Is there~~   No, there isn't.
> No, there isn't.   Yes, there is.   Is there

Now listen and repeat.

13.11 Look at the picture and write the correct answers in the spaces.

> Yes, there are.
> No, there aren't.
>
> ~~Yes, there are.~~
> No, there aren't.
>
> No, there aren't.
> Yes, there are.

Are there any plants in the garden?

Yes, there are.

❶ Are there any flowers in the kitchen?

_____

❷ Are there any windows in the dining room?

_____

❸ Are there any clocks in the bedroom?

_____

❹ Are there any chairs in the dining room?

_____

❺ Are there any armchairs in the living room?

_____

Now listen and repeat.

103

14 Review: Where I live

 14.1 Listen and read.

I'm Andy and this is my town.

In my town, there's a hospital and a school. There are two parks and three stores.

That's my house. I live next to the hospital.

14.2 Write about your town then draw your house and town.

I'm _____ and this is my town.

In my town, there's a _____ and a _____. There are _____ and _____.

That's my house. I live _____ the _____.

15 On the farm

15.1 Listen and write the correct words in the spaces.

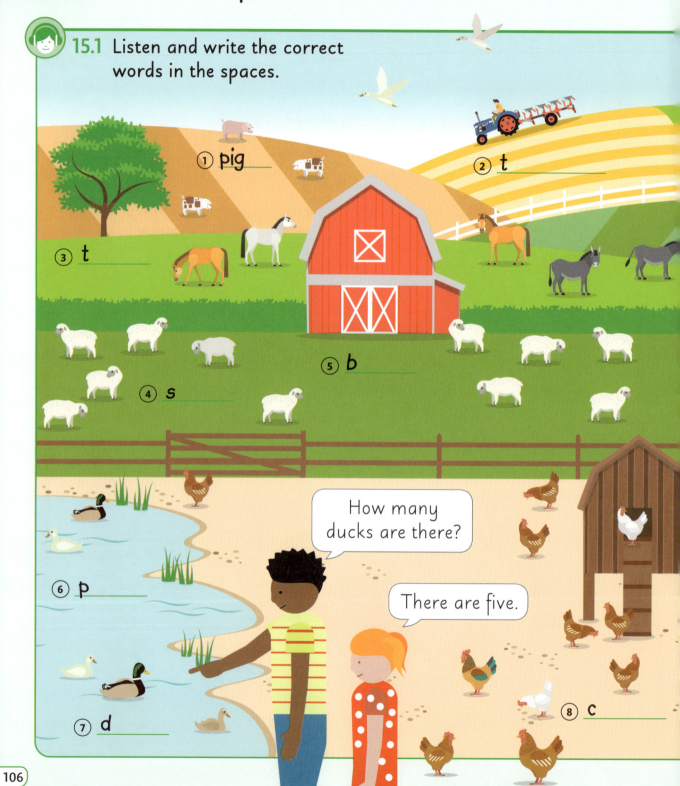

106

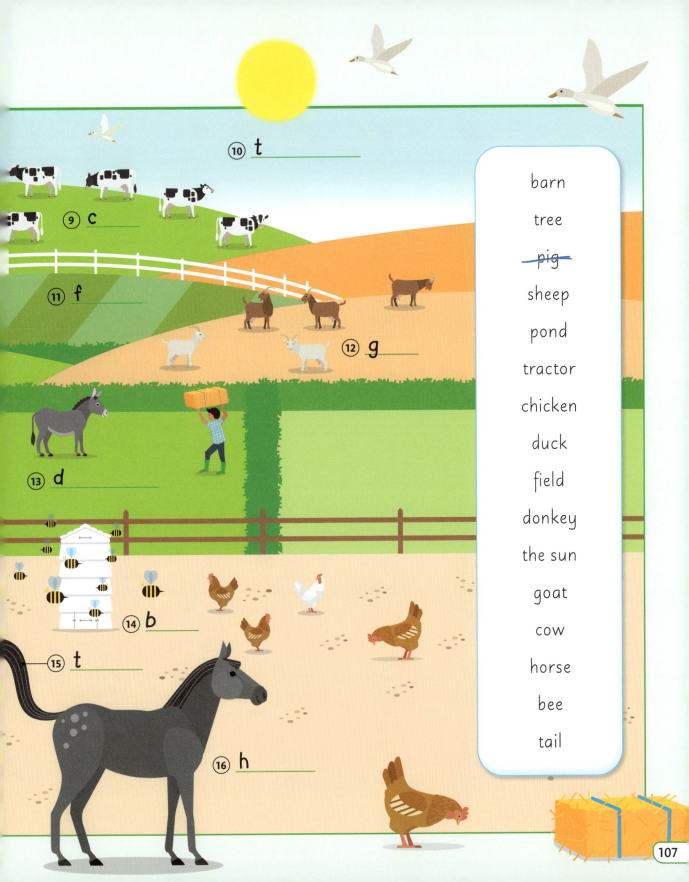

15.2 Find and circle the five words in the grid.

tail   donkey   ~~barn~~
pig   bee   horse

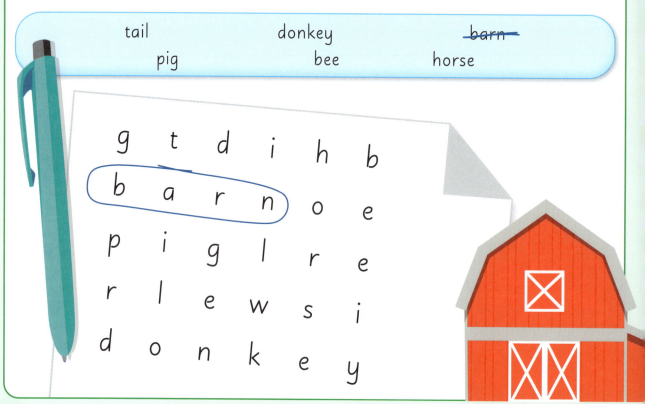

15.3 Listen and check off the correct pictures.

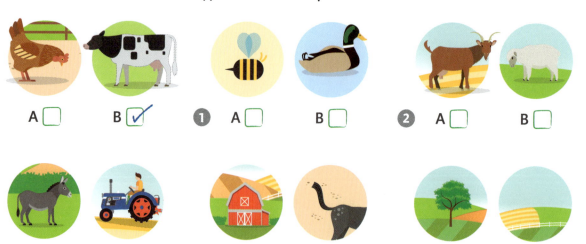

15.4 Look at the pictures and circle the correct words.

(bee) / goat

1 donkey / pond

2 sheep / tractor

3 the sun / horse

4 duck / tail

5 tree / chicken

Now listen and repeat.

15.5 Look at the pictures and write the correct words in the spaces.

barn   goat   ~~chicken~~
donkey   field   sheep

 chicken

1  _____

2  _____

3  _____

4  _____

5 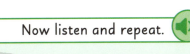 _____

Now listen and repeat.

109

15.6 Look at the picture and match the questions to the correct answers.

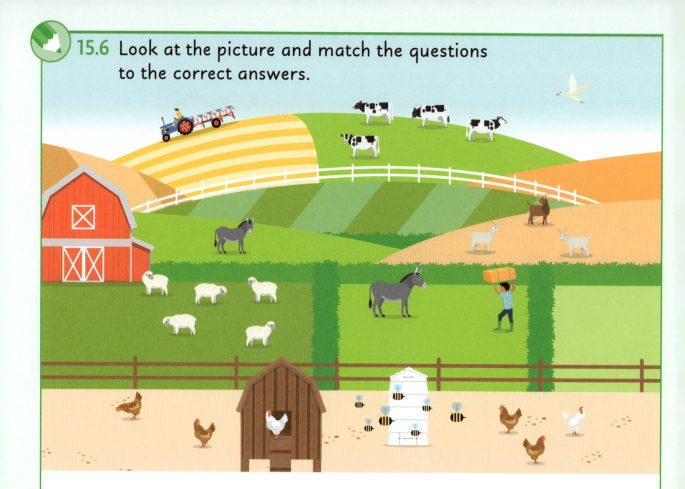

How many barns are there?   There are five.

❶ How many sheep are there?   There are three.

❷ How many cows are there?   There are six.

❸ How many goats are there?   There's one.

❹ How many bees are there?   There are two.

❺ How many chickens are there?   There are four.

❻ How many donkeys are there?   There are seven.

Now listen and repeat.

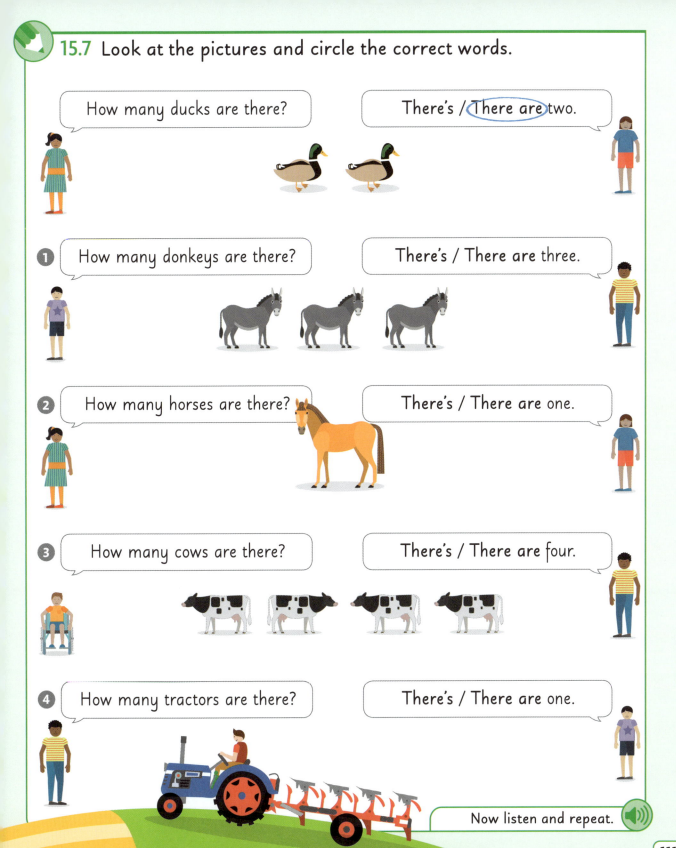

15.8 **Look at the pictures and write the correct words in the spaces.**

| behind | ~~in~~ | next to | in front of |

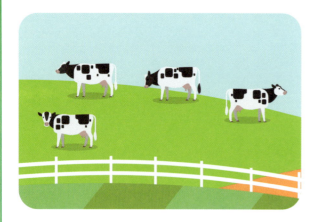

Where are the cows?

They're ____in____ the field.

❶ Where's the horse?

It's _____ the tree.

❷ Where's the donkey?

It's _____ the pond.

❸ Where are the goats?

They're _____ the barn.

Now listen and repeat.

112

15.9 Listen to the song and write the correct words in the spaces.

Where are the _ducks_ ?
They're in the _____ !

Where are the _____ ?
They're _____ the field!

Where are the _____ ?
They're in the _____ !

_____ are the animals?
They're _____ my farm!

15.10 Look at the pictures and check off the correct sentences.

The donkey's in the field. ☑
The donkeys are in the field. ☐

The duck's in the pond. ☐
The ducks are in the pond. ☐

The sheep's in front of the barn. ☐
The sheep are in front of the barn. ☐

The horse is under the tree. ☐
The horses are under the tree. ☐

Now listen and repeat.

113

16 Sports

16.1 Listen and write the correct words in the spaces.

① basketball
② b_____
③ s_____
④ t_____

~~basketball~~   baseball
table tennis   ice hockey
tennis   soccer
swimming   badminton

5 b
6 s
7 t
8 i

16.2 Write the correct words under the pictures.

b a s e b a l l

b _ _ _ _ _ _ _ _

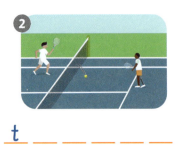

t _ _ _ _ _ _

s _ _ _ _ _ _ _ _

Now listen and repeat.

16.3 Listen and check off the correct pictures.

A ☐ B ✓ ① A ☐ B ☐ ② A ☐ B ☐

③ A ☐ B ☐ ④ A ☐ B ☐ ⑤ A ☐ B ☐

116

16.4 **Look at the pictures and write the correct words in the spaces.**

swim   play tennis   ~~run~~   bounce   throw
catch   kick   play ice hockey   hit   jump

run

1 j

2 s

3 p

4 p

5 c

6 b

7 k

8 t

9 h

Now listen and repeat.

117

16.5 Look at the pictures and circle the correct words.

run / hit   swim / run

jump / kick   catch / bounce   throw / hit

Now listen and repeat.

16.6 Read the words and check off the correct pictures.

jump   ① play tennis   ② run

A ☐   B ✓   A ☐   B ☐   A ☐   B ☐

③ bounce   ④ play basketball   ⑤ throw

A ☐   B ☐   A ☐   B ☐   A ☐   B ☐

Now listen and repeat.

118

16.7 Look at the pictures and write the correct words in the spaces.

jump   catch   ~~kick~~
throw   bounce

16.8 Match the pictures to the correct words.

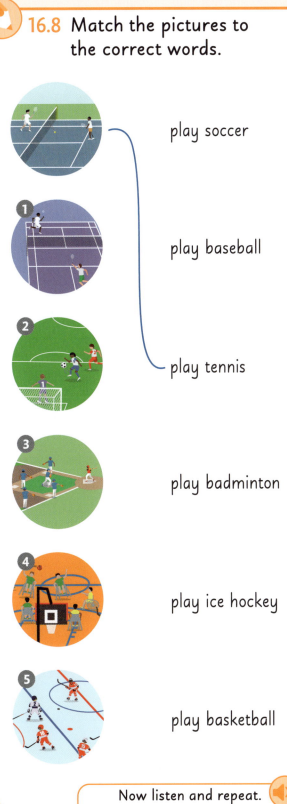

Now listen and repeat.   Now listen and repeat.

16.9 Listen and write the correct words in the spaces.

can't   can   ~~can't~~   can   can't   can   can't

I __can't__ play table tennis.

1. I _____ play tennis.

2. I _____ play baseball.

3. I _____ play ice hockey.

4. I _____ play basketball.

5. I _____ play badminton.

6. I _____ play soccer.

16.10 Listen and check off the correct answers.

Can you bounce a ball?   Yes, I can.

No, I can't. ☐

1 Can you swim?  Yes, I can. ☐

No, I can't. ☐

2 Can you play basketball?   Yes, I can. ☐

No, I can't. ☐

3 Can you throw a ball?   Yes, I can. ☐

No, I can't. ☐

4 Can you play soccer?  Yes, I can. ☐

No, I can't. ☐

16.11 **Look at the pictures and write the correct words in the spaces.**

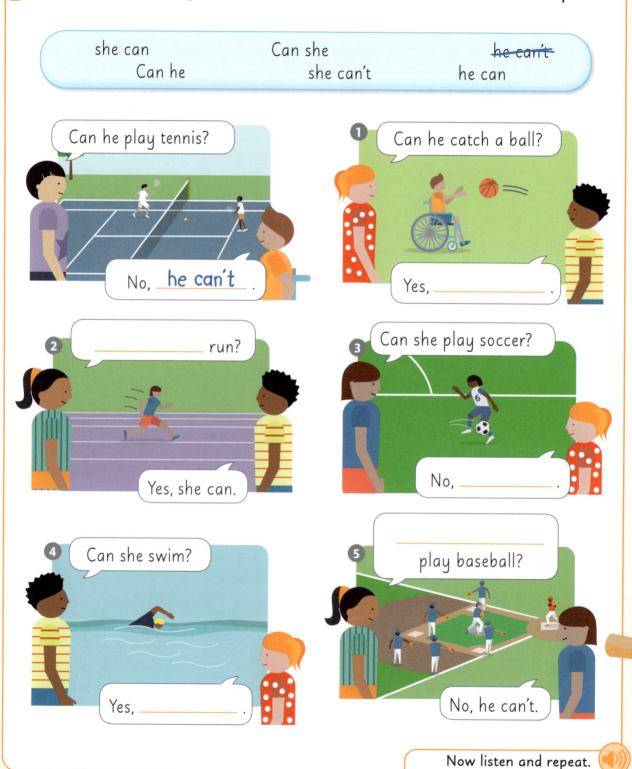

Now listen and repeat.

16.12 Listen and match the questions to the correct answers.

Can Max swim? — Yes, he can.

❶ Can she play table tennis? — No, she can't.

❷ Can Maria play badminton? — Yes, she can.

❸ Can he play ice hockey? — No, he can't.

16.13 There are four sentences. Mark the beginning and end of each one and write them below.

Can she play baseball?

❶ _____

❷ _____

❸ _____

Cansheplaybaseball?Yes,shecan.Canheswim?No,hecan't.

Now listen and repeat.

17 At the food market

17.1 Listen and write the correct words in the spaces.

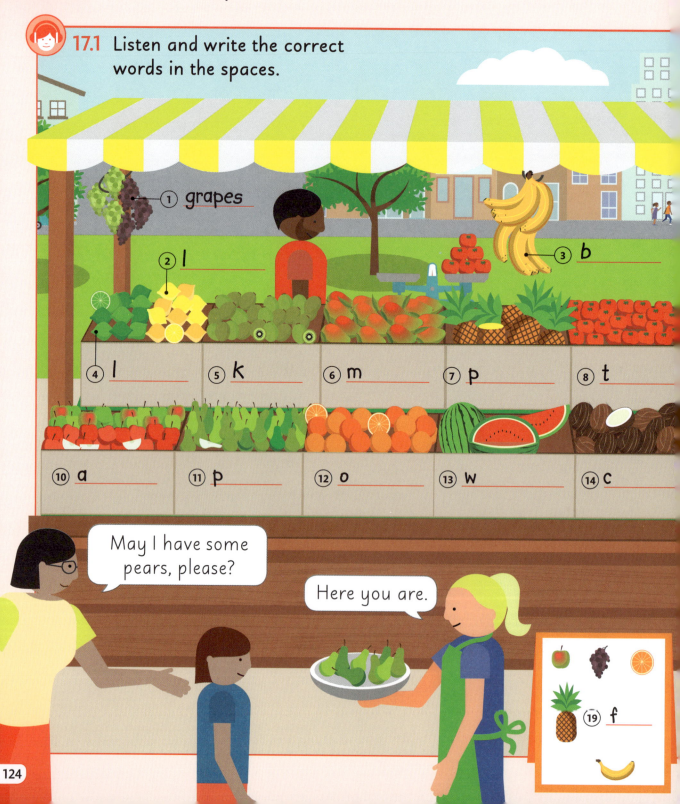

125

17.2 **Look at the pictures and write the letters in the correct order.**

o i n s n o   k w i s i   p r a e s

o n i o n s   ① k _ _ _ _ _   ② p _ _ _ _

a p l p s e   f u t r i   g p r a e s

③ a _ _ _ _ _   ④ f _ _ _ _   ⑤ g _ _ _ _ _

l m e s i   m t a e   l m e n s o

⑥ l _ _ _ _   ⑦ m _ _ _   ⑧ l _ _ _ _ _

Now listen and repeat.

126

17.3 Match the pictures to the correct words.

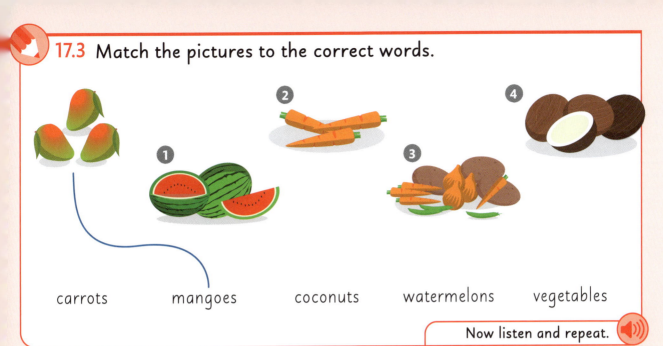

carrots   mangoes   coconuts   watermelons   vegetables

Now listen and repeat.

17.4 Listen to the song and write the correct words in the spaces.
17.5 Color in the three foods that you heard in the song.

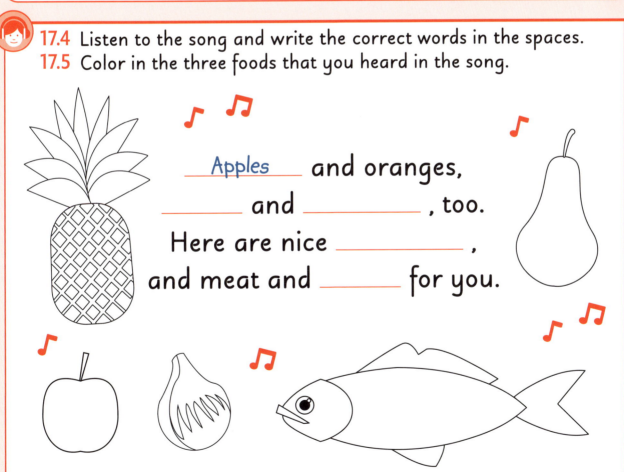

___Apples___ and oranges,
_____ and _____, too.
Here are nice _____,
and meat and _____ for you.

17.6 Look at the pictures and write the correct words in the spaces.

> or   ~~don't like~~   and   like   and   or

I __don't like__ pears or oranges.

❶ I like tomatoes _____ carrots.

❷ I don't like potatoes _____ onions.

❸ I _____ lemons and limes.

❹ I don't like apples _____ coconuts.

❺ I like mangoes _____ watermelons.

Now listen and repeat.

128

17.7 Listen and check off the correct answers.

Do you like pineapples?

Yes, I do. ✓

No, I don't. ☐

1. Do you like potatoes?

Yes, I do. ☐

No, I don't. ☐

2. Do you like grapes?

Yes, I do. ☐

No, I don't. ☐

3. Do you like meat?

Yes, I do. ☐

No, I don't. ☐

4. Do you like bananas?

Yes, I do. ☐

No, I don't. ☐

17.9 Read the questions and check off the correct pictures.

May I have some tomatoes, please?

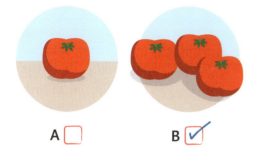

A ☐   B ✓

❶ May I have a potato, please?

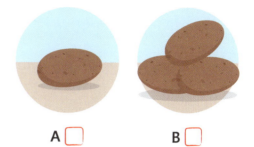

A ☐   B ☐

❷ May I have some coconuts, please?

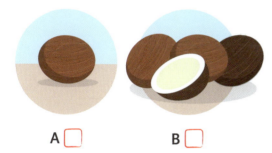

A ☐   B ☐

❸ May I have an apple, please?

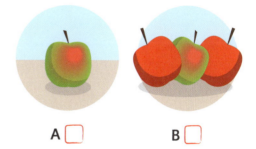

A ☐   B ☐

❹ May I have a kiwi, please?

A ☐   B ☐

❺ May I have some bananas, please?

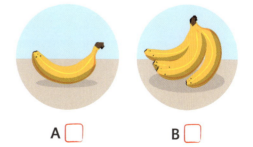

A ☐   B ☐

Now listen and repeat.

131

18 At the toy store

18.1 Listen and write the correct words in the spaces.

ball
action figure
~~alien~~
teddy bear
monster
doll
puppet
car
board game
train
rocket
video game
the moon
balloons
stars
robot

TOYS

9 r_____   10 t_____

11 s_____

13 b_____

12 r_____

14 t_____

15 v_____

16 b_____

It's Ben's birthday.

Let's give him a robot.

18.2 Listen and check off the correct pictures.

18.3 Look at the pictures and write the letters in the correct order.

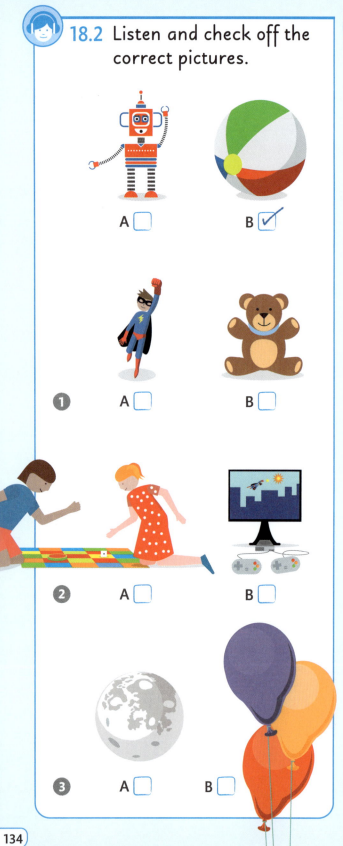

Now listen and repeat.

18.4 Look at the pictures and circle the correct words.

(doll) / ball

1. car / teddy bear

2. the moon / train

3. board game / monster

4. alien / puppet

Now listen and repeat.

18.5 Look at the pictures and write the correct words in the spaces.

monster   ~~stars~~   robot   car

stars

1. _____

2. _____

3. _____

Now listen and repeat.

18.6 Listen and write the correct answers in the spaces.

No, she doesn't.   ~~Yes, he does.~~
    Yes, she does.   No, he doesn't.

Does he like aliens?   Yes, he does.

1 Does she like board games?

2 Does she like video games?

3 Does he like robots?

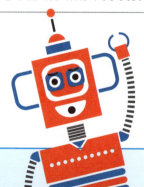 

136

18.7 Look at the pictures and circle the correct words.

Ben (likes) / doesn't like trains.

1 She likes / doesn't like puppets.

2 Maria likes / doesn't like aliens.

3 He likes / doesn't like cars.

4 Sara likes / doesn't like rockets.

5 Max likes / doesn't like monsters.

6 He likes / doesn't like dolls.

7 She likes / doesn't like balloons.

Now listen and repeat.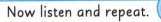

18.8 Listen and check off the correct answers.

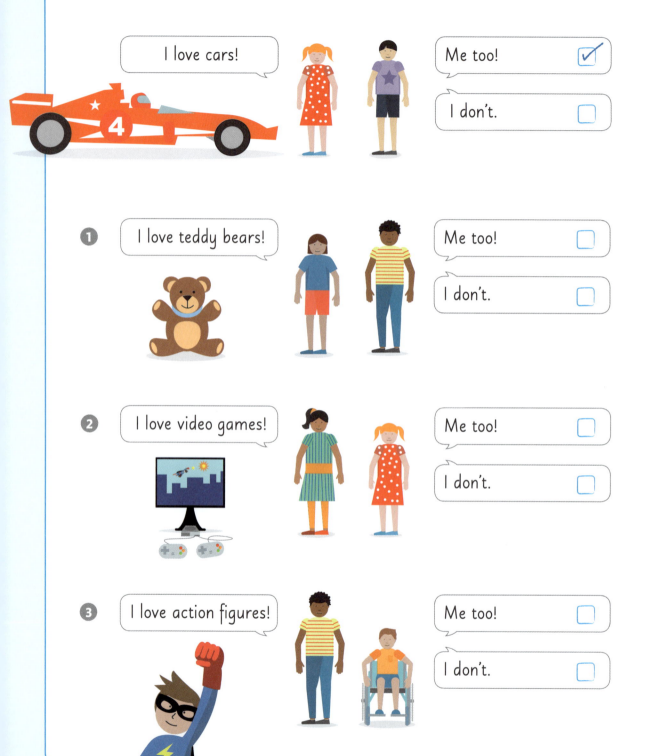

18.9 Listen to the song and write the correct words in the spaces.
18.10 Color in the three toys that you heard in the song.

Maria likes __dolls__ ,
but she doesn't like _____ .
Andy likes _____ ,
but he doesn't like _____ .
I like _____ and video games,
and my favorite toy
is my _____ !

19 Our hobbies

19.1 Listen and write the correct words in the spaces.

- draw pictures
- ~~ride a bike~~
- paint
- skateboard
- watch soccer
- play the guitar
- read
- take photos
- play the piano
- dance
- sing

① ride a bike
② w
③ s
④ d
⑤ p

I enjoy painting.
Me too. It's fun!

19.2 Read the words and check off the correct pictures.

play the guitar
A ✓ B ☐

① read
A ☐ B ☐

② draw pictures
A ☐ B ☐

③ dance
A ☐ B ☐

④ take photos
A ☐ B ☐

⑤ skateboard
A ☐ B ☐

Now listen and repeat.

19.3 Look at the pictures and circle the correct words.

read / (ride a bike)

①  dance / skateboard

② play the piano / read

③  sing / paint

④  watch soccer / sing

Now listen and repeat.

142

19.4 **Match the pictures to the correct words.**

ride a bike   play the piano   draw pictures   take photos   play the guitar

Now listen and repeat.

19.5 **Look at the pictures and write the letters in the correct order.**

 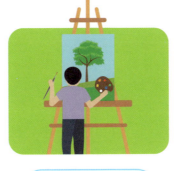 

d n e c a   p n t a i   r d e a

d a n c e   ① p _ _ _ _   ② r _ _ _

s g n i

③ s _ _ _

Now listen and repeat.

143

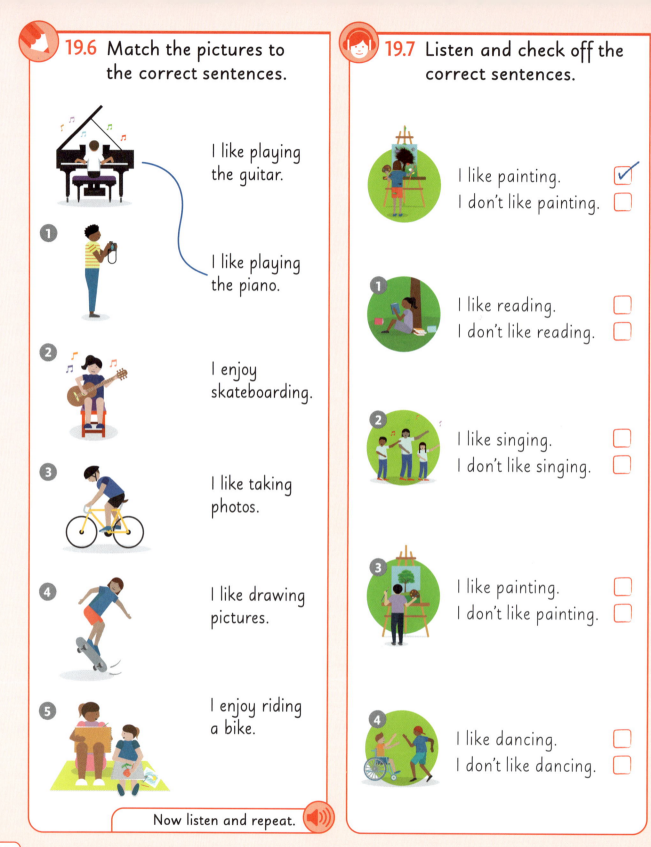

19.8 Look at the pictures and write the correct words in the spaces.

> drawing pictures   ~~painting~~   reading   taking photos   riding a bike

I enjoy __painting__.

1. I like _____.

2. I like _____.

3. I enjoy _____.

4. I like _____.

Now listen and repeat.

19.9 There are four sentences. Mark the beginning and end of each one and write them below.

__Do you like reading?__

1. _____

2. _____

3. _____

Doyoulikereading?|Yes,Ido.Doyoulikesinging?No,Idon't.

Now listen and repeat.

19.10 Look at the pictures and write the correct words in the spaces.

> I don't   ~~Do you like~~   reading
> I do   Do you like   No

Now listen and repeat.

19.11 Listen and write the correct answers in the spaces.

> ~~Yes, I do.~~   No, I don't.
> Yes, I do.   No, I don't.
>   Yes, I do.

Do you like reading?
Yes, I do.

① Do you like riding a bike?
_____

② Do you like playing the guitar?
_____

③ Do you like singing?
_____

④ Do you like painting?
_____

19.12 Listen to the song and write the correct words in the spaces.

Do you have hobbies?
Yes, I do.
I __love__ reading books and skateboarding, too.

Do you like playing _____?
Yes, I do.
I love _____ tennis and playing _____, too.

Do you _____ singing?
Yes, I do.
I love _____ songs, and I love _____, too.

147

20 Review: What I like

 20.1 Listen and read.

I'm Andy. I enjoy playing tennis. I like oranges and pears, but I don't like tomatoes. I love video games.

My friend Eva enjoys playing table tennis. She likes watermelons, but she doesn't like pears. My friend loves robots.

20.2 Write about the things you and a friend like then draw a picture.

I'm _____ . I enjoy _____ .
I like _____ and _____ ,
but I don't like _____ .
I love _____ .

My friend _____ enjoys _____ .
_____ likes _____ , but
_____ doesn't like _____ .
My friend loves _____ .

21 Our party clothes

21.1 Listen and write the correct words in the spaces.

21.2 Look at the pictures and circle the correct words.

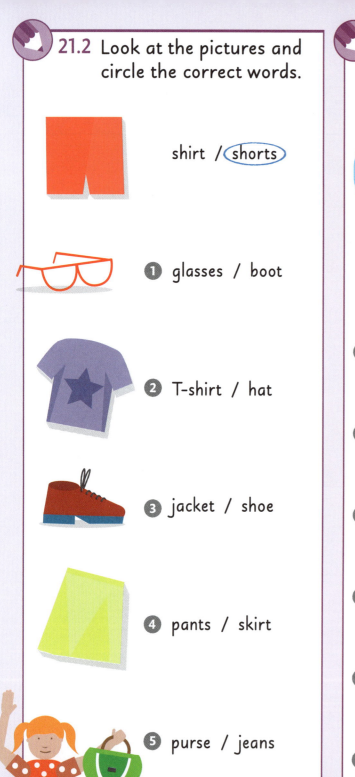

shirt / (shorts)

1. glasses / boot
2. T-shirt / hat
3. jacket / shoe
4. pants / skirt
5. purse / jeans

Now listen and repeat.

21.3 Look at the pictures and write the correct words in the spaces.

shirt ~~hat~~ jeans dress watch shorts jacket

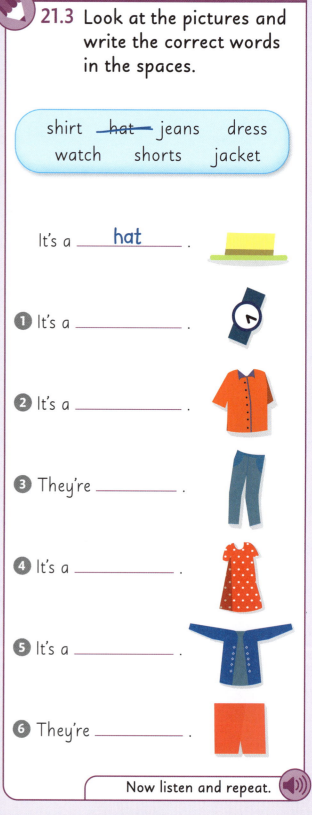

It's a ___hat___ .

1. It's a _____ .
2. It's a _____ .
3. They're _____ .
4. It's a _____ .
5. It's a _____ .
6. They're _____ .

Now listen and repeat.

21.4 Listen and check off the correct pictures.

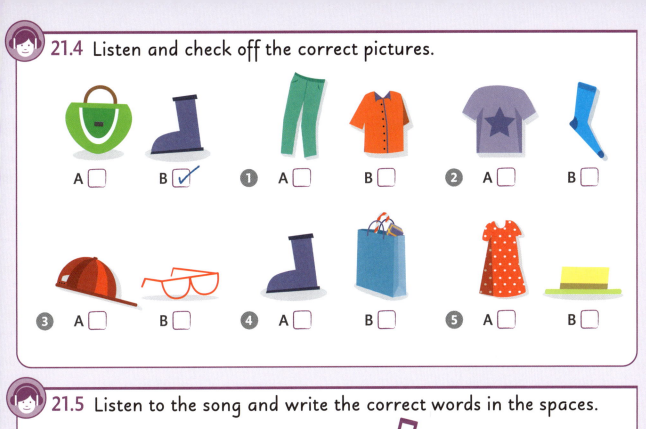

21.5 Listen to the song and write the correct words in the spaces.

We're at a ___party___,
so let's all _____ and play.
What a fun _____
for Ben's birthday!

Andy's _____ his
favorite _____,
and Sara has
a beautiful _____.

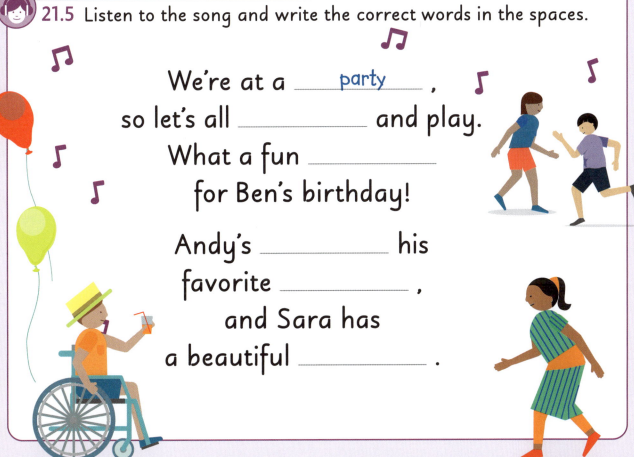

21.6 **Look at the pictures and check off the correct sentences.**

I'm wearing socks. ☐
I'm wearing glasses. ✓

I'm wearing a jacket. ☐
I'm wearing pants. ☐

I'm wearing a hat. ☐
I'm wearing a watch. ☐

I'm wearing a watch. ☐
I'm wearing jeans. ☐

I'm wearing a dress. ☐
I'm wearing boots. ☐

I'm wearing pants. ☐
I'm wearing a hat. ☐

Now listen and repeat.

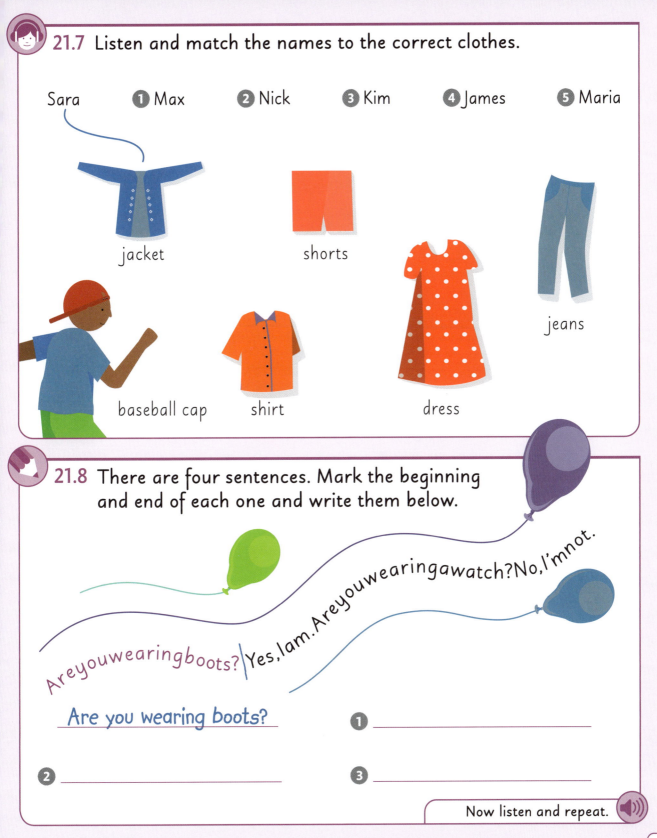

21.9 Look at the pictures and write the correct answers in the spaces.

No, I'm not.   ~~Yes, I am.~~   No, I'm not.   Yes, I am.

Are you wearing my baseball cap?

Yes, I am.

1. Are you wearing my pants?

2. Are you wearing my shirt?

3. Are you wearing my boots?

Now listen and repeat.

21.10 Look at the pictures and circle the correct words.

(What a) / What lovely watch!

① What a / What clean shoes!

② What a / What dirty jeans!

③ What a / What nice hat!

④ What a / What colorful bag!

⑤ What a / What nice skirt!

Now listen and repeat.

21.11 Match the pictures to the correct sentences.

 ①  ②  ③ ④

What lovely pants!   What a nice watch!   What dirty socks!

What a beautiful dress!   What lovely shorts!

Now listen and repeat.

157

22 Our day at the beach

22.1 Listen and write the correct words in the spaces.

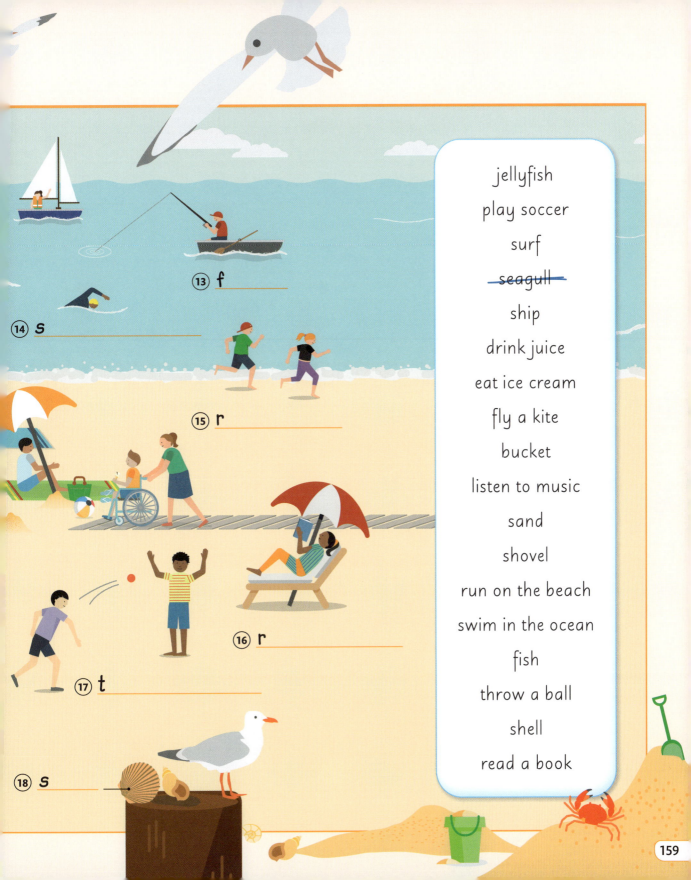

22.2 Match the pictures to the correct words.

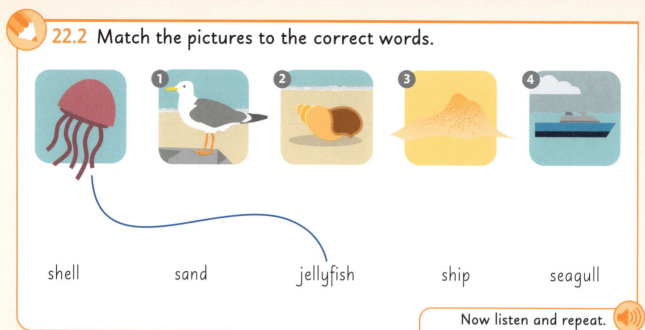

shell   sand   jellyfish   ship   seagull

Now listen and repeat.

22.3 Listen and color in the pictures.

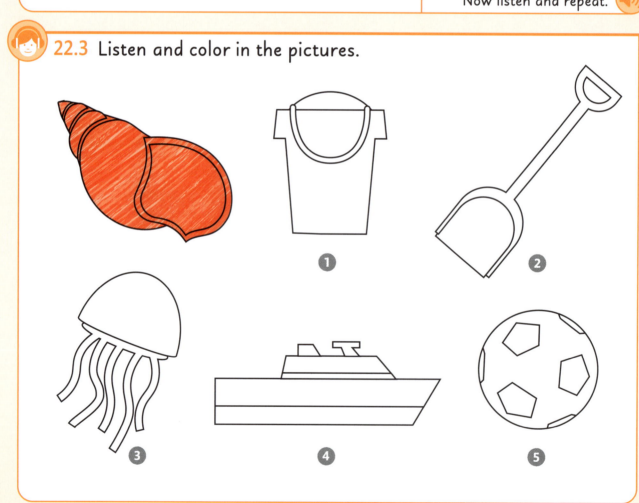

22.4 Read the sentences and check off the correct pictures.

I'm listening to music.

A ✓   B ☐

1 I'm fishing.

A ☐   B ☐

2 I'm playing soccer.

A ☐   B ☐

3 I'm reading a book.

A ☐   B ☐

4 I'm throwing a ball.

A ☐   B ☐

5 I'm running on the beach.

A ☐   B ☐

6 I'm surfing.

A ☐   B ☐

7 I'm swimming in the ocean.

A ☐   B ☐

Now listen and repeat.

22.5 Look at the pictures and circle the correct words.

(She's)/ She isn't reading a book.

❶ He's / He isn't swimming.

❷ He's / He isn't listening to music.

❸ She's / She isn't drinking juice.

❹ She's / She isn't surfing.

❺ He's / He isn't flying a kite.

❻ She's / She isn't running.

Now listen and repeat.

22.6 Look at the pictures and write the correct words in the spaces.

surfing   ~~throwing~~   playing   listening   drinking   reading

He's __throwing__ a ball.

❶ She's _____ juice.

❷ She's _____ .

❸ He's _____ soccer.

❹ She's _____ a book.

❺ He's _____ to music.

Now listen and repeat.

163

22.7 Look at the pictures and check off the correct answers.

Is Peter fishing?
- Yes, he is. ✓
- No, he isn't. ☐

1. Is he reading a book?
- Yes, he is. ☐
- No, he isn't. ☐

2. Is he flying a kite?
- Yes, he is. ☐
- No, he isn't. ☐

3. Is she playing soccer?
- Yes, she is. ☐
- No, she isn't. ☐

4. Is Maria eating ice cream?
- Yes, she is. ☐
- No, she isn't. ☐

Now listen and repeat.

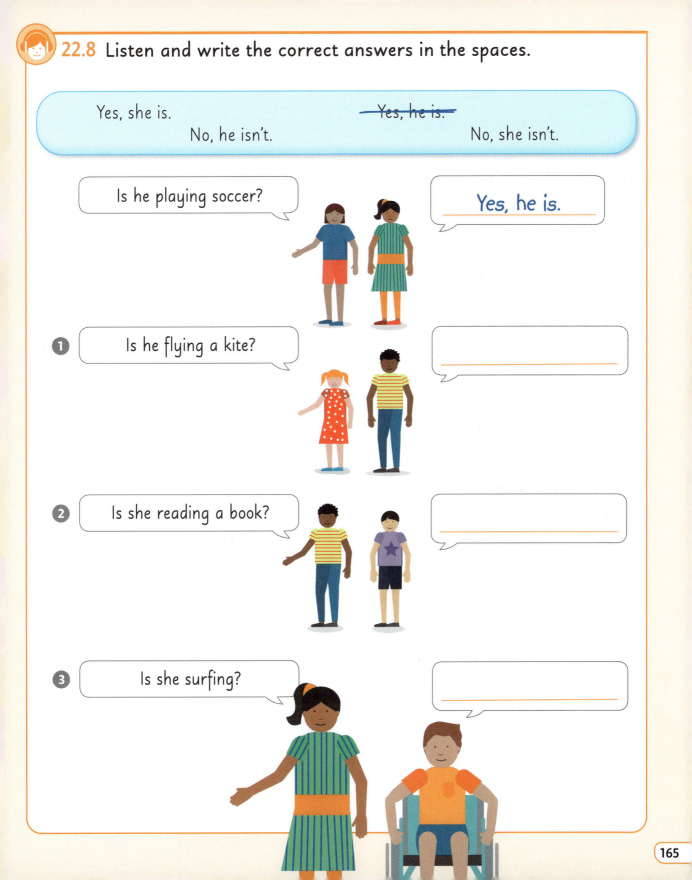

23 Lunchtime

23.1 Listen and write the correct words in the spaces.

23.2 Match the pictures to the correct words.

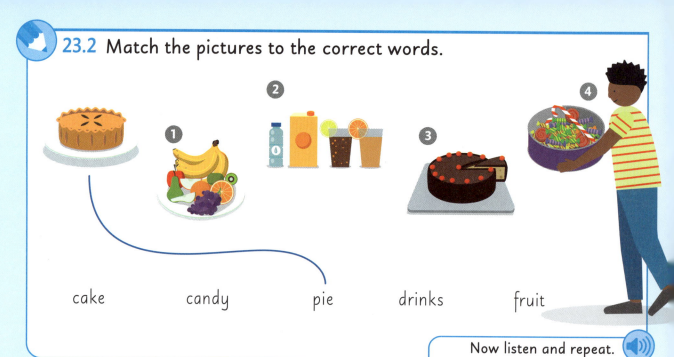

cake   candy   pie   drinks   fruit

Now listen and repeat.

23.3 Look at the pictures and write the words in the correct place on the crossword.

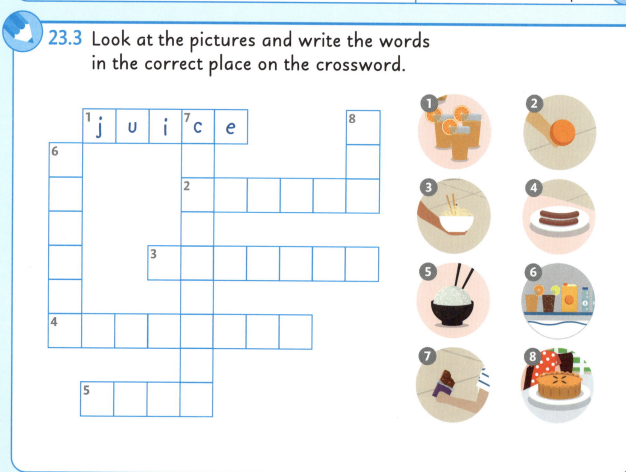

23.4 **Listen and match the questions to the correct answers.**

What would you like?

I'd like some fries, please.

1. What would you like?

I'd like some water, please.

2. What would you like?

I'd like an orange, please.

3. What would you like?

I'd like a burger, please.

4. What would you like?

I'd like some lemonade, please.

169

23.5 Look at the pictures and circle the correct words.

I'd like **a /(some)** fruit, please.

❶ I'd like **a / some** juice, please.

❷ I'd like **a / some** rice, please.

❸ I'd like **an / some** orange, please.

❹ I'd like **a / some** burger, please.

❺ I'd like **a / some** noodles, please.

Now listen and repeat.

23.6 Listen and write the correct words in the spaces.

> No, I wouldn't.   No, thank you.   ~~Yes, I would.~~
> Yes, please.   Yes, I would.

 Would you like some chocolate? <u>Yes, I would.</u>

1. Would you like a drink? _____

2.  Would you like some salad?  _____

3.  Would you like some fries? _____

4. Would you like some cake?  _____

23.7 Listen and write the correct words in the spaces.

egg	lunch	potatoes	~~breakfast~~	bread
pasta		rice	meatball	chicken
beans	fish	milk	dinner	peas

23.8 Listen and match the questions to the correct answers.

What's for breakfast today, Mom?   Meat and potatoes.
① What's for lunch today, Dad?   Chicken and peas.
② What's for breakfast today, Dad?   Fish and beans.
③ What's for dinner today, Mom?   Eggs and bread.
④ What's for lunch today, Mom?   Meatballs and rice.
⑤ What's for dinner today, Dad?   Milk and bread.

23.9 There are four sentences. Mark the beginning and end of each one and write them below.

What'sforlunch?/Fishandpotatoes.What'sfordinner?Pastaandmeatballs.

_____ What's for lunch?

① _____

② _____

③ _____

Now listen and repeat.

173

24 At the park

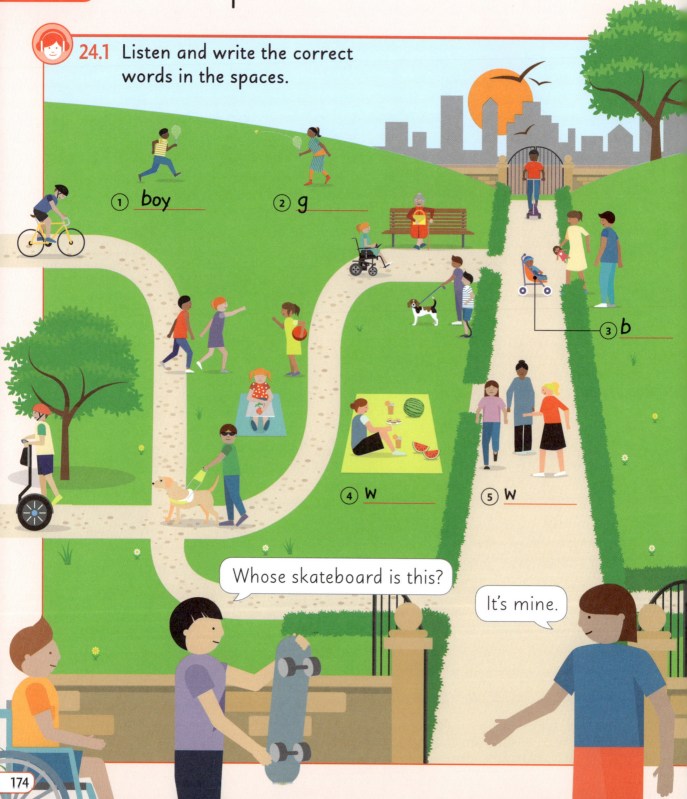

24.1 Listen and write the correct words in the spaces.

① boy
② g
③ b
④ w
⑤ w

Whose skateboard is this?

It's mine.

baby woman girl ~~boy~~
women child/kid person men
children/kids man people

⑥ p _____ ⑦ p _____
⑧ c _____ ⑨ c _____
⑩ m _____ ⑪ m _____

175

24.4 **Match the pictures to the correct words.**

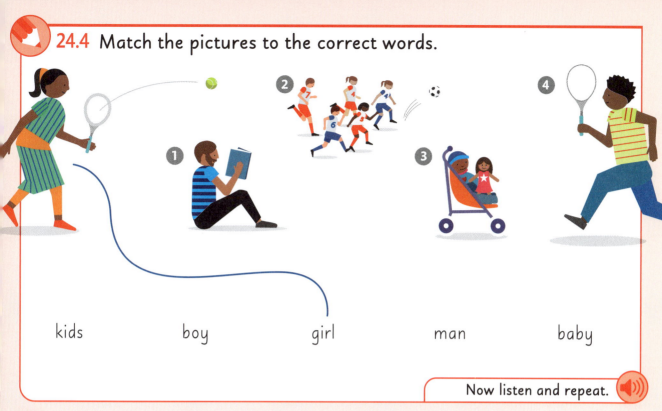

kids　　　　boy　　　　girl　　　　man　　　　baby

Now listen and repeat.

24.5 **Read the words and check off the correct pictures.**

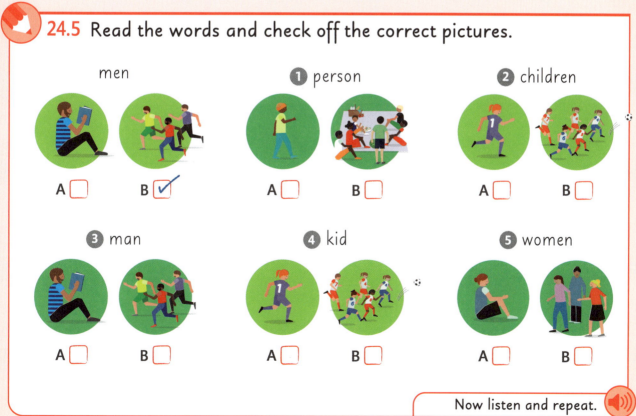

Now listen and repeat.

24.6 Rewrite the questions in the correct order.

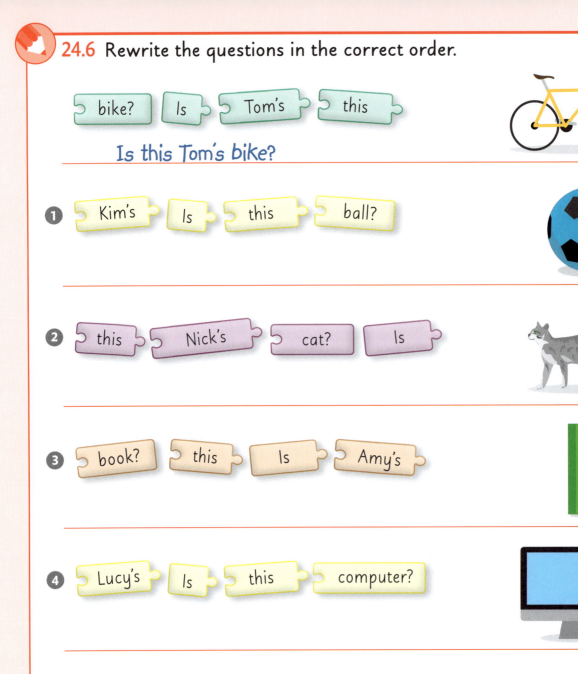

Is this Tom's bike?

1. Is this Kim's ball?

2. Is this Nick's cat?

3. Is this Amy's book?

4. Is this Lucy's computer?

5. Is this Maria's jacket?

Now listen and repeat.

24.7 Listen and write the correct names in the spaces.
24.8 Listen again and color in the pictures.

Kim   Sam   ~~Sara~~
   Ann   Andy   Matt

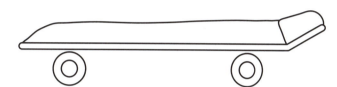

Sara

1 _____

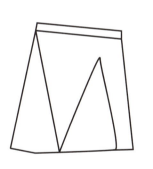

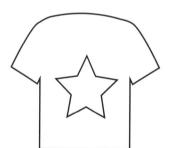

2 _____   3 _____   4 _____

5 _____

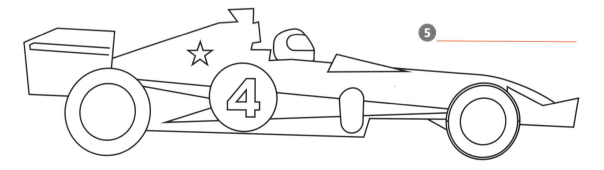

24.9 Listen and check off the correct answers.

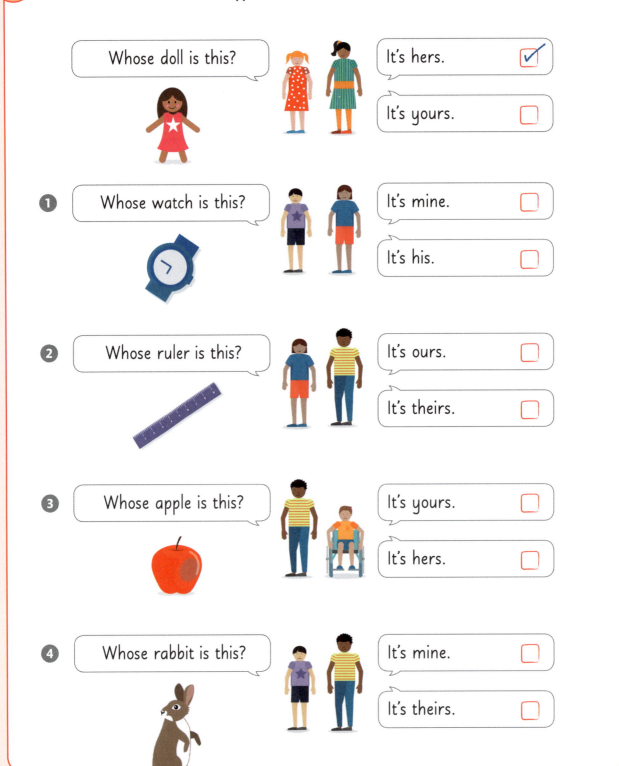

24.10 Listen and circle the correct words.

Whose bucket is this?

It's (mine) / theirs.

❶ Whose camera is this?

It's his / hers.

❷ Whose tortoise is this?

It's ours / theirs.

❸ Whose purse is this?

It's hers / mine.

❹ Whose juice is this?

It's yours / his.

❺ Whose bike is this?

It's mine / theirs.

❻ Whose skateboard is this?

It's hers / ours.

❼ Whose ball is this?

It's ours / yours.

25 My day

25.1 Listen and write the correct sentences in the spaces.

① I get up.

⑫ I g _____

I eat dinner.	I call my friend.
I go swimming.	
~~I get up.~~	I go to sleep.

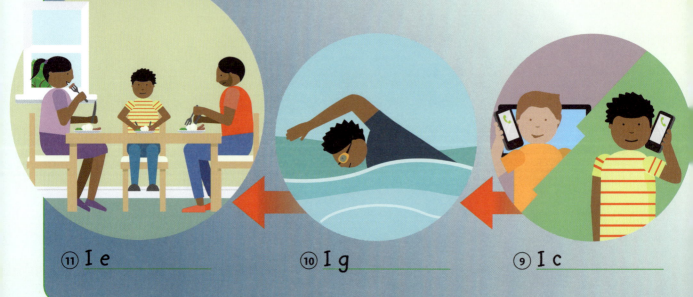

⑪ I e _____   ⑩ I g _____   ⑨ I c _____

② I m _____ ③ I e _____ ④ I b _____

I go home.   I make my bed.
I walk to school.   I eat breakfast.
I brush my teeth.
I eat lunch.   I study English.

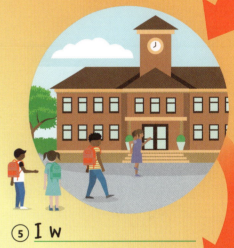

⑤ I w _____

⑧ I g _____ ⑦ I e _____ ⑥ I s _____

25.2 Look at the pictures and check off the correct sentences.

I walk to school. ☐
I eat breakfast. ☑

I go home. ☐
I call my friend. ☐

I get up. ☐
I make my bed. ☐

I brush my teeth. ☐
I eat dinner. ☐

I go swimming. ☐
I walk to school. ☐

I go to sleep. ☐
I study English. ☐

Now listen and repeat.

25.3 Rewrite the sentences in the correct order.

bed. | my | make | I

I make my bed.

1. call | my | I | friend.

2. to | walk | school. | I

3. sleep. | go | I | to

4. my | brush | teeth. | I

5. eat | I | lunch.

Now listen and repeat.

25.4 Look at the clocks and write the correct answers in the spaces.

It's five o'clock. It's six o'clock. ~~It's two o'clock.~~
It's nine o'clock. It's ten o'clock. It's three o'clock.
It's eleven o'clock. It's four o'clock. It's one o'clock.

What time is it?
It's two o'clock.

❶ What time is it?

❷ What time is it?

❸ What time is it?

❹ What time is it?

❺ What time is it?

❻ What time is it?

❼ What time is it?

❽ What time is it?

Now listen and repeat.

186

25.5 Match the pictures to the correct words.

In the afternoon   At night   In the morning   In the evening

Now listen and repeat.

25.6 Listen and circle the correct words.

I go swimming in the morning / (afternoon).

I walk to school in the morning / evening.

I eat dinner in the afternoon / evening.

I go home in the morning / afternoon.

I go to sleep at night / afternoon.

I make my bed in the evening / morning.

187

25.7 Read the sentences and write the correct words in the spaces.

in   ~~eight o'clock~~   morning   When do you   at   four o'clock

When do you walk to school?

I walk to school at __eight o'clock__.

1 _____ get up?

I get up at seven o'clock.

2 When do you eat dinner?

I eat dinner _____ the evening.

3 When do you go to sleep?

I go to sleep _____ eight o'clock.

4 When do you go home?

I go home at _____.

5 When do you brush your teeth?

I brush my teeth in the _____ and at night.

Now listen and repeat.

25.8 Look at the pictures and check off the correct sentences.

He goes to sleep.
He go to sleep. ☐

We walks to school. ☐
We walk to school. ☐

She calls her friend. ☐
She call her friend. ☐

He brushes his teeth. ☐
He brush his teeth. ☐

They eats dinner. ☐
They eat dinner. ☐

I goes home. ☐
I go home. ☐

Now listen and repeat.

189

25.9 Write the letters in the correct order.

M d n o a y
M o n d a y

① T s d u y e a
T _ _ _ _ _ _ _

② W d n e a s e y d
W _ _ _ _ _ _ _ _ _

③ T u r a s y h d
T _ _ _ _ _ _ _ _

④ F i d y r a
F _ _ _ _ _

⑤ S u t a d y a r
S _ _ _ _ _ _ _

⑥ S d n a y u
S _ _ _ _ _

Now listen and repeat.

25.10 Read the sentences and circle the correct words.

I walk to school (at) / on seven o'clock.

① I go swimming at / on Tuesdays.

② I call my friend at / on Fridays.

③ I eat lunch at / on twelve o'clock.

Now listen and repeat.

190

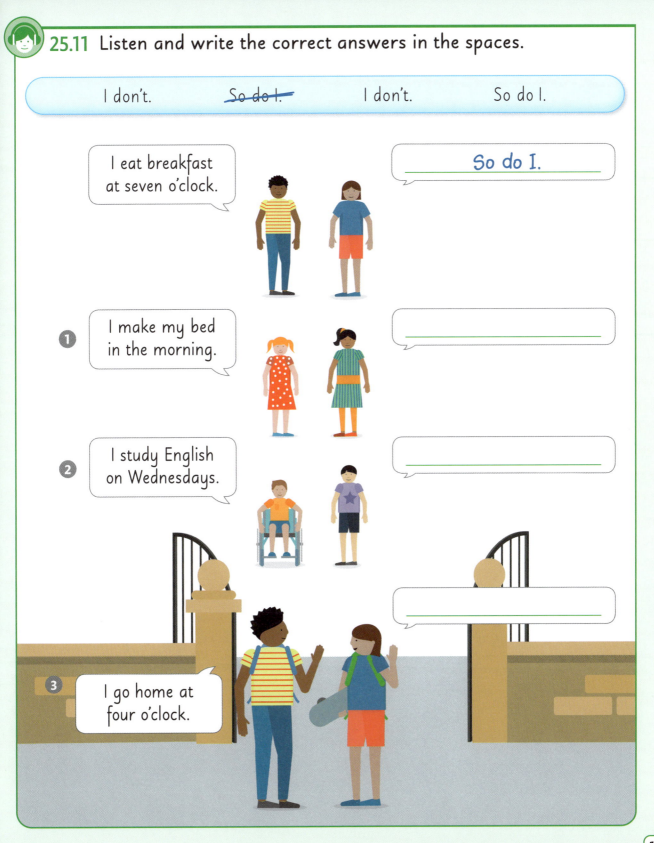

26 Review: Me and my day

 26.1 Listen and read.

My name's Maria. Today I'm wearing a dress and shoes. My favorite food is cake and I love burgers, too.

I get up at 7 o'clock and I eat breakfast.
In the evening, I call my friend.
I study English on Tuesdays.
On Saturdays, I go swimming.

26.2 Write about the things you do then draw a picture of your favorite foods.

My name's _____ . Today I'm wearing _____ and _____ . My favorite food is _____ and I love _____ , too.

I get up at _____ and I _____ .
In the evening, I _____ .
I study English on _____ .
On Saturdays, I _____ .

Handwriting guide

A1 To practice writing English letters, start at the red dot and then follow the arrows.

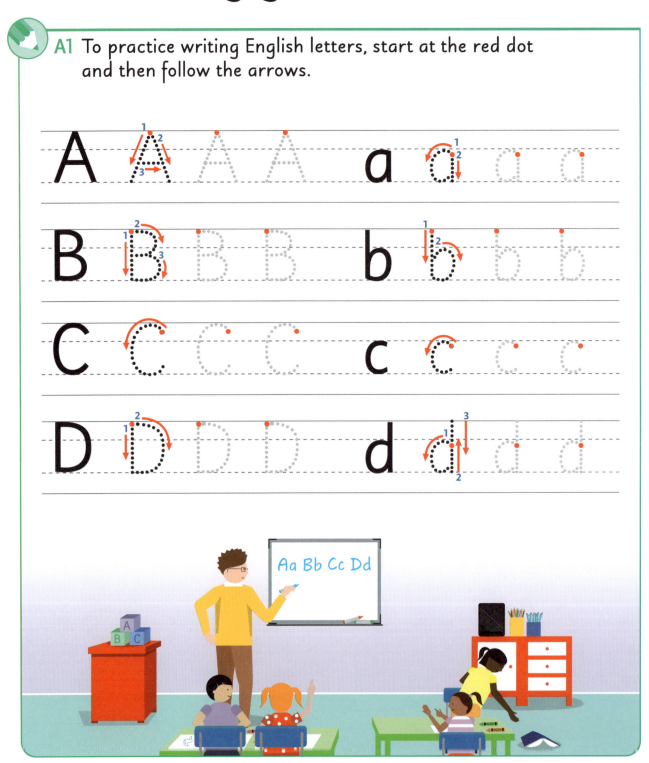

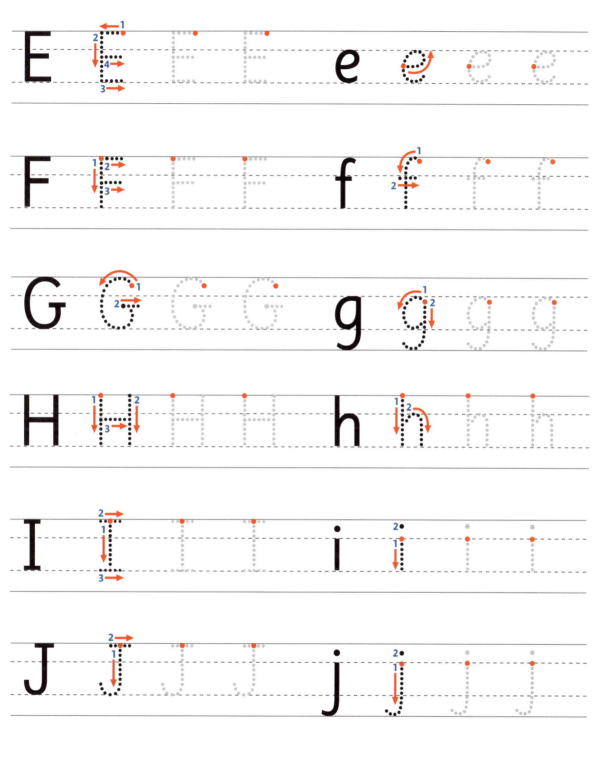

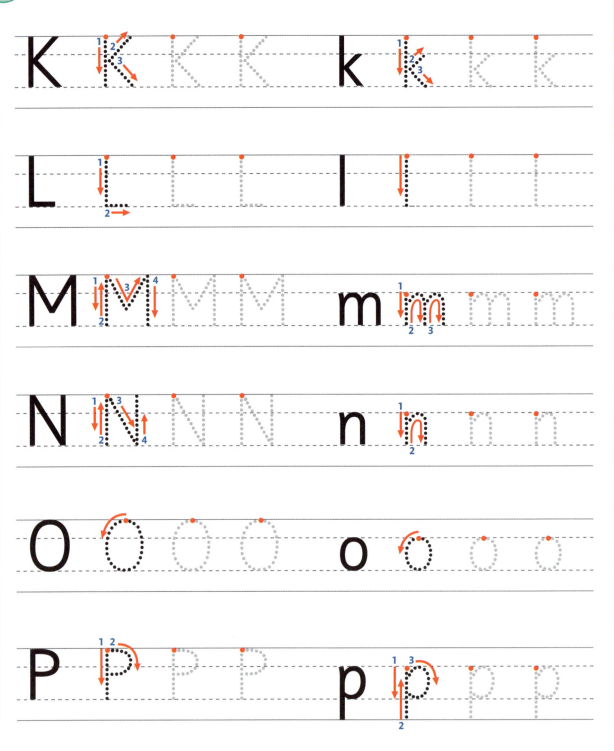

Q q

R r

S s

T t

U u

V v

197

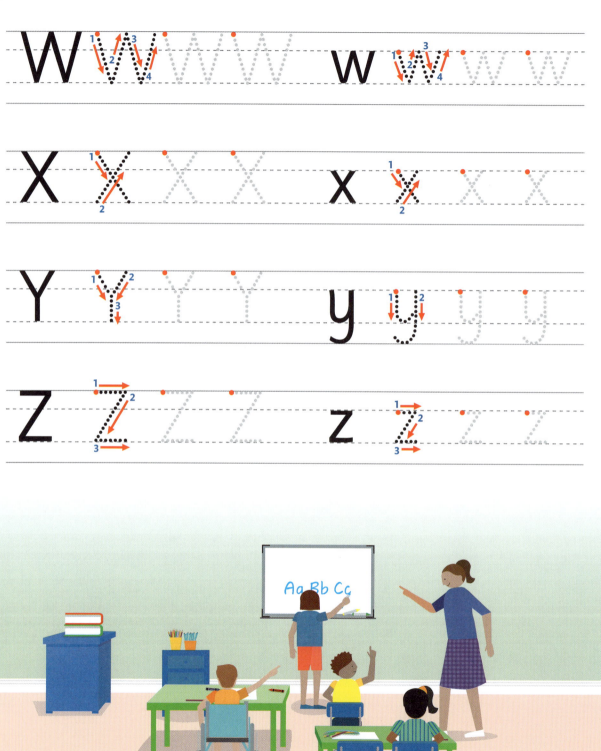

Answers

1

1.1
1. Maria 2. Ben 3. Max
4. Andy 5. Sofia 6. Sara

1.2
1. Hi, my **name's** Sara.
2. Hi, I'm **Max**.
3. Hi, **I'm** Andy.
4. Hello, I'm **Maria**.
5. **Hello**, I'm Ben.

1.3

1.4
1. Andy 2. Sara 3. Max
4. Maria 5. Sofia

1.5
1. three 2. seven 3. nine
4. six 5. ten 6. eight
7. five

1.6
1. eight 2. two 3. four
4. one 5. seven

1.7
1. one 2. two 3. five
4. four 5. six

1.8
1. I'm fine, thanks.
2. I'm nine years old.

2

2.1
1. playground 2. numbers
3. letters 4. teacher
5. board 6. classmate
7. alphabet 8. tablet
9. cupboard 10. book

2.2
1. tablet 2. teacher
3. alphabet 4. board

5 playground   6 letters
7 numbers   8 classmate
9 cupboard

2.3
1 cupboard   2 numbers
3 tablet   4 teacher
5 board   6 book

2.4
1 A   2 B   3 A   4 A   5 B

2.5
1 pick up   2 sit down
3 find   4 stand up
5 ask

2.6
1 show   2 listen   3 close
4 find   5 answer

2.7
1 find   2 ask   3 show
4 look   5 open   6 close
7 add   8 answer

2.8
1 **His** name's Andy.
2 **His** name's Ben.
3 **Her** name's Maria.

4 **His** name's Max.
5 **Her** name's Sofia.

2.9
1 His name's Dan.
2 Her name's Bella.
3 His name's Tom.
4 Her name's Anna.
5 Her name's Amy.

2.10
1 Her name's Evie.
2 What's his name?
3 His name's Jack.

3

3.1
1 write   2 read   3 count
4 play   5 spell   6 paint
7 draw

3.2
1 read   2 play   3 write
4 paint

3.3
1 A   2 A   3 B   4 A   5 A

3.4

1. Let's write!
2. Let's count!
3. Let's paint!
4. Let's read!
5. Let's play!

3.5

Hello, **hello**!
What's your **name**?
How are you?
Let's **play** a game.

Let's say hello
to my new friends
Max and Maria,
Sara and **Ben**.

3.6

1. twelve
2. sixteen
3. fifteen
4. twenty

3.7

1. fourteen
2. nineteen
3. eighteen
4. eleven
5. sixteen
6. twenty
7. thirteen
8. fifteen

3.8

1. tablet
2. numbers
3. cars
4. dog
5. cupboard

3.9

1. A
2. B
3. B
4. B

4

4.1

1. pink
2. book
3. crayon
4. eraser
5. pen
6. paper
7. ball
8. notepad
9. purple
10. red
11. book pack
12. ruler
13. white
14. brown
15. apple
16. orange
17. green
18. yellow
19. blue
20. pencil
21. gray
22. black
23. watch

4.2

1. crayon
2. eraser
3. pen
4. pencil
5. watch

4.3

1. green
2. pink
3. brown
4. black
5. gray

4.4
1. purple
2. book pack
3. white
4. notepad
5. orange
6. yellow
7. paper

4.5
1. A
2. A
3. A
4. B
5. B

4.6
1. It's a watch.
2. It's a ball.
3. They're rulers.

4.7
1. What are **these**?
2. It's an **apple**.
3. **It's** a pencil.
4. **What are** these?
5. **They're** notepads.

4.8

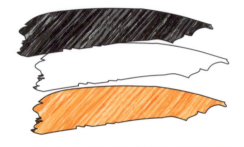

4.9
1. B
2. A
3. B
4. A

4.10
1. It's purple.
2. It's red.
3. It's orange.

5

5.1
1. zebra
2. giraffe
3. lion
4. elephant
5. hippo
6. parrot
7. tiger
8. monkey

⑨ bear
⑩ frog
⑪ snake
⑫ polar bear
⑬ bird
⑭ whale
⑮ penguin
⑯ crocodile
⑰ lizard

5.2
① hippo
② parrot
③ tiger
④ elephant
⑤ crocodile

5.3
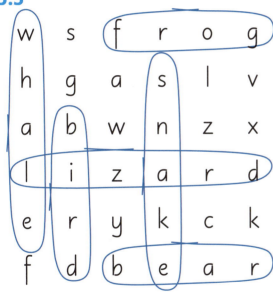

5.4
① whale
② lion
③ zebra
④ bear

5.5
Animals, animals
everywhere!
a **lion**, a giraffe,
and a **polar bear**.

A **whale** and
a **penguin**,
a tiger and a **snake**,
animals, animals,
they are great!

5.6
① What's **that**? ② **They're** hippos.
③ **What's** that?

5.7
① It's a zebra. ② It's a crocodile.
③ They're parrots.

5.8
① It's a lizard.
② They're penguins.
③ It's a parrot.
④ They're elephants.
⑤ It's a bird.

5.9
① They're tigers. ② What's that?
③ It's an elephant.

203

5.10
1. A 2. A 3. B 4. B 5. A

5.11
1. My favorite animal is a **lizard**.
2. My favorite animal is a **bear**.
3. My favorite animal is a **bird**.
4. My favorite animal is an **elephant**.
5. My favorite animal is a **monkey**.

6

6.1
1. my family
2. my grandmother/grandma
3. my grandfather/grandpa
4. my father/dad
5. my mother/mom
6. my brother
7. my sister
8. me
9. my uncle
10. my aunt
11. my cousin

6.2
1. my grandma
2. my cousin
3. my family
4. my uncle
5. my grandpa

6.3
1. brother
2. mother
3. grandfather
4. sister

6.4
1. She's my **cousin**.
2. He's my **uncle**.
3. She's my **sister**.
4. He's my **dad**.
5. She's my **grandma**.

6.5
1. No, he isn't.
2. No, she isn't.
3. Yes, she is.

6.6
1. doctor
2. teacher
3. chef
4. firefighter

6.7
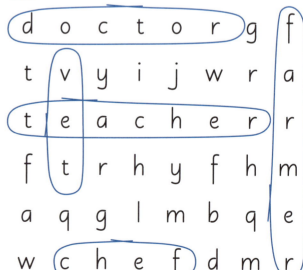

204

6.8

1 She's a **doctor**.
2 He's a **teacher**.
3 She's a **chef**.
4 She's a **police officer**.

6.9

1 She's a doctor.
2 She's a chef.
3 He's a farmer.
4 She's a teacher.
5 She's a police officer.

6.10

Who's this?
She's my **mother**.
Who's that?
He's my **brother**.

My **dad** is a teacher,
my **mom** is a vet,
Grandpa's a **doctor**,
And Grandma's a **chef**!

7

7.1

1 poster
2 computer
3 mouse
4 keyboard

5 lamp
6 toy box
7 desk
8 doll
9 chair
10 car
11 camera
12 rug
13 bed
14 teddy bear
15 baseball bat
16 ball
17 skateboard
18 tennis racket

7.2

1 skateboard
2 chair
3 toy box
4 car
5 lamp

7.3

1 A   2 B   3 B   4 A

7.4

1 B   2 A   3 B   4 B   5 A

7.5

1 doll
2 skateboard
3 toy box
4 computer

7.6

1 **That's** my ball.
2 **These are** my cameras.
3 **Those are** my teddy bears.
4 **That's** my toy box.
5 **This is** my tennis racket.

7.7

1. Andy
2. Andy
3. Andy
4. Maria
5. Maria
6. Andy
7. Maria

7.8

1. No, I don't.
2. Yes, I do.
3. Yes, I do.
4. No, I don't.

7.9

1. No, I don't.
2. Yes, I do.
3. No, I don't.
4. Yes, I do.
5. No, I don't.

7.10

This is my **toy box**
and these are my **toys**,
I have a **ball**
and a **skateboard**, too.
Toys are fantastic!
Toys are cool!

9

9.1

1. tired
2. hungry
3. thirsty
4. scared
5. hot
6. cold
7. excited
8. sad
9. happy

9.2

1. cold
2. scared
3. hungry
4. sad
5. hot

9.3

1. A
2. A
3. B
4. B
5. A

9.4

1. thirsty
2. tired
3. happy
4. excited

9.5

Are you **happy**?
Yes, we are!
We are at the fair.

Are you **tired**?
No, we aren't.
We aren't tired
or **scared**!

9.6
1. We're happy.
2. We're thirsty.
3. We're really hot.

9.7
1. We're happy.
2. They're cold.
3. They're hot.
4. We're sad.
5. They're thirsty.
6. They're tired.
7. We're scared.

9.8
1. We're really **excited**.
2. They're **hot**.
3. We're **happy**.
4. We're **really** tired.

9.9
1. Yes, we are.
2. Yes, we are.
3. No, they're not.
4. No, we're not.
5. Yes, they are.

9.10
1. Yes, they are.
2. Yes, we are.

3. No, we're not.
4. No, they're not.

9.11
1. No, they're not.
2. No, we're not.
3. Yes, they are.
4. No, they're not.
5. No, we're not.
6. Yes, we are.
7. Yes, they are.

10

10.1
1. rabbit
2. tortoise
3. dog
4. mouse
5. collar
6. spider
7. cat
8. vet
9. fish

10.2
1. old
2. nice
3. scary
4. dirty
5. clean
6. beautiful
7. big
8. small

10.3
1 rabbit 2 fish
3 spider 4 collar

10.4
1 cat 2 vet 3 mouse
4 dog 5 tortoise

10.5
1 A 2 A 3 B 4 B

10.6

I have a **cat**,
she's **black** and **small**.
She likes to run
and play with a ball.

Maria has a **tortoise**,
his name is Socks.
He's **old** and **green**
and he's in this box.

10.7
1 Sara has a tortoise.
2 Ben has a rabbit.
3 She has a fish.
4 She has a cat.
5 He has a cat.

10.8
1 B 2 B 3 B 4 A 5 B

10.9
1 Yes, he does.
2 Yes, she does.
3 No, he doesn't.

10.10
1 A 2 A 3 B 4 A 5 B

10.11
1 The mouse.
2 Which one is scary?
3 The spider!

11

11.1
1 hair 2 nose
3 face 4 long hair
5 mouth 6 body
7 hand 8 arm
9 fingers 10 leg
11 toes 12 foot
13 feet 14 head
15 short hair 16 eye
17 ear 18 teeth

11.2

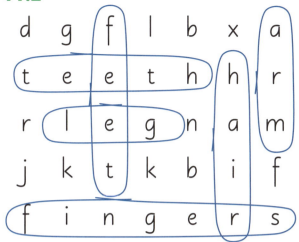

11.3
1. long hair
2. ear
3. teeth
4. body

11.4
1. mouth
2. nose
3. head
4. foot
5. hand

11.5
1. A
2. B
3. B

11.6
1. The robot has **purple** eyes.
2. It has red **teeth**.
3. It has purple **legs**.
4. The robot has **blue** feet.
5. It has a **yellow** nose.
6. The robot has orange **hands**.

11.7

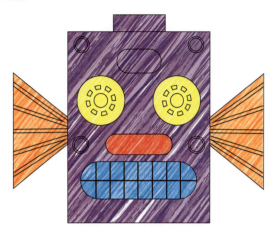

11.8
1. Yes, it does.
2. No, it doesn't.
3. No, it doesn't.
4. Yes, it does.
5. No, it doesn't.

11.9
1. No, it doesn't.
2. Yes, it does.
3. No, it doesn't.
4. Yes, it does.
5. Yes, it does.

11.10
1. clap
2. touch
3. move
4. point

209

11.11

Clap your hands,
touch your nose,
move your feet,
point your toes!

Point one finger,
move your head,
wave your arms,
touch one leg!

12

12.1

1. airport
2. airplane
3. street
4. train
5. bike
6. zoo
7. park
8. bookstore
9. lake
10. boat
11. helicopter
12. school
13. fire station
14. apartment block
15. hospital
16. house
17. store
18. truck
19. car
20. bus
21. motorcycle

12.2

1. bus
2. school
3. bike
4. hospital
5. truck

12.3

1. A 2. B 3. A 4. B 5. A

12.4

1. car
2. train
3. lake
4. park

12.5

This is my town,
there's a park
and a zoo.
There's an airport,
a lake, and
a fire station, too.

This is my town,
there are cars and
a school.
This is my town,
I love it, it's cool.

12.6

1. There are two stores.
2. There's a fire station.
3. There's a zoo.
4. There are three houses.
5. There are four cars.

12.7

1. A 2. B 3. B 4. A 5. A

12.8
1. in front of
2. between
3. next to

12.9
1. It's **behind** the green car.
2. It's **in front of** the lake.
3. It's **next to** the school.
4. It's **between** the hospital and the bookstore.
5. It's **in front of** the hospital.

12.10
1. It's behind the school.
2. It's between the airport and the apartment block.
3. It's next to the lake.
4. It's behind the hospital.
5. It's between the fire station and the store.

13

13.1
1. garden
2. bedroom
3. clock
4. plants
5. wall
6. window
7. floor
8. armchair
9. bookcase
10. bathroom
11. mirror
12. bath
13. living room
14. television/TV
15. couch
16. hall
17. door
18. mat
19. lights
20. kitchen
21. refrigerator
22. dining room
23. flowers
24. table
25. chair

13.2
1. dining room
2. living room
3. kitchen
4. bedroom
5. hall

13.3
1. armchair
2. window
3. table
4. lights

13.4
1. couch
2. door
3. refrigerator

13.5
1. clock
2. bookcase
3. chair
4. plants

13.6
1. on
2. under

13.7
1. The cat is **in** the bath.
2. The plants are **under** the window.
3. The cat is **on** the mat.
4. The bookcase is **under** the lights.
5. The flowers are **on** the table.

13.8
1. A 2. B 3. A 4. A

13.9
The TV's **in**
the living room,
the **mat** is in the **hall**.

Where's the **clock**?
It's **on** my
bedroom **wall**.

13.10
1. No, there isn't.
2. Yes, there is.
3. No, there isn't.
4. Yes, there is.
5. **Is there** a table in the dining room?

13.11
1. No, there aren't.
2. No, there aren't.
3. Yes, there are.
4. Yes, there are.
5. No, there aren't.

15

15.1
1. pig
2. tractor
3. tree
4. sheep
5. barn
6. pond
7. duck
8. chicken
9. cow
10. the sun
11. field
12. goat
13. donkey
14. bee
15. tail
16. horse

15.2
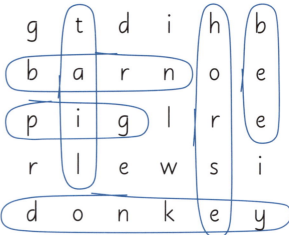

15.3
1. B 2. A 3. B 4. A 5. B

15.4

1 pond 2 tractor 3 the sun
4 tail 5 tree

15.5

1 field
2 barn
3 donkey
4 sheep
5 goat

15.6

1 There are five.
2 There are four.
3 There are three.
4 There are seven.
5 There are six.
6 There are two.

15.7

1 **There are** three.
2 **There's** one.
3 **There are** four.
4 **There's** one.

15.8

1 It's **behind** the tree.
2 It's **next to** the pond.
3 They're **in front of** the barn.

15.9

Where are the **ducks**?
They're in the **pond**!

Where are the **goats**?
They're **in** the field!

Where are the **cows**?
They're in the **barn**!

Where are the animals?
They're **on** my farm!

15.10

1 The ducks are in the pond.
2 The sheep are in front of the barn.
3 The horse is under the tree.

16

16.1

1 basketball 2 baseball
3 soccer 4 tennis
5 badminton 6 swimming
7 table tennis 8 ice hockey

16.2

1 badminton 2 tennis
3 swimming

213

16.3
1 B 2 A 3 B 4 B 5 B

16.4
1 jump 2 swim
3 play tennis 4 play ice hockey
5 catch 6 bounce
7 kick 8 throw
9 hit

16.5
1 swim 2 kick
3 catch 4 hit

16.6
1 A 2 A 3 B 4 B 5 B

16.7
1 throw
2 jump
3 bounce
4 catch

16.8
1 play badminton
2 play soccer
3 play baseball
4 play basketball
5 play ice hockey

16.9
1 I **can** play tennis.
2 I **can't** play baseball.
3 I **can't** play ice hockey.
4 I **can** play basketball.
5 I **can't** play badminton.
6 I **can** play soccer.

16.10
1 No, I can't.
2 No, I can't.
3 Yes, I can.
4 Yes, I can.

16.11
1 Yes, **he can**.
2 **Can she** run?
3 No, **she can't**.
4 Yes, **she can**.
5 **Can he** play baseball?

16.12
1 Yes, she can.
2 No, she can't.
3 Yes, he can.

16.13
1 Yes, she can.
2 Can he swim?
3 No, he can't.

17

17.1
1. grapes
2. lemons
3. bananas
4. limes
5. kiwis
6. mangoes
7. pineapples
8. tomatoes
9. onions
10. apples
11. pears
12. oranges
13. watermelons
14. coconuts
15. carrots
16. potatoes
17. meat
18. fish
19. fruit
20. vegetables

17.2
1. kiwis
2. pears
3. apples
4. fruit
5. grapes
6. limes
7. meat
8. lemons

17.3
1. watermelons
2. carrots
3. vegetables
4. coconuts

17.4
Apples and oranges,
pears and mangoes, too.
Here are nice potatoes,
and meat and fish for you.

17.5

17.6
1. I like tomatoes **and** carrots.
2. I don't like potatoes **or** onions.
3. I **like** lemons and limes.
4. I don't like apples **or** coconuts.
5. I like mangoes **and** watermelons.

17.7
1. Yes, I do.
2. No, I don't.
3. No, I don't.
4. Yes, I do.

17.8

1. May I have **some** onions, please?
2. May I have **a** lemon, please?
3. May I have **some** pears, please?
4. May I have **an** orange, please?
5. May I have **some** carrots, please?

17.9

1. A   2. B   3. A   4. A   5. B

18

18.1

1. alien
2. puppet
3. teddy bear
4. action figure
5. ball
6. doll
7. monster
8. car
9. rocket
10. the moon
11. stars
12. robot
13. balloons
14. train
15. video game
16. board game

18.2

1. A   2. B   3. B

18.3

1. doll   2. ball   3. train
4. stars

18.4

1. teddy bear
2. the moon
3. board game
4. puppet

18.5

1. monster
2. car
3. robot

18.6

1. No, she doesn't.
2. Yes, she does.
3. No, he doesn't.

18.7

1. She **doesn't like** puppets.
2. Maria **likes** aliens.
3. He **doesn't like** cars.
4. Sara **likes** rockets.
5. Max **likes** monsters.
6. He **doesn't like** dolls.
7. She **likes** balloons.

18.8

1. I don't.
2. Me too!
3. I don't.

18.9

Maria likes **dolls**,
but she doesn't like **puppets**.
Andy likes **cars**,
but he doesn't like **rockets**.
I like **trains** and video games,
and my favorite toy
is my **monster**!

18.10

19

19.1
1. ride a bike
2. watch soccer
3. skateboard
4. draw pictures
5. paint
6. read
7. sing
8. dance
9. play the guitar
10. play the piano
11. take photos

19.2
1. B 2. B 3. A 4. A 5. A

19.3
1. skateboard
2. play the piano
3. sing
4. watch soccer

19.4
1. play the guitar
2. take photos
3. ride a bike
4. play the piano

19.5
1. paint
2. read
3. sing

19.6
1. I like taking photos.
2. I like playing the guitar.
3. I enjoy riding a bike.
4. I enjoy skateboarding.
5. I like drawing pictures.

19.7

1. I like reading.
2. I don't like singing.
3. I don't like painting.
4. I like dancing.

19.8

1. I like **drawing pictures**.
2. I like **riding a bike**.
3. I enjoy **taking photos**.
4. I like **reading**.

19.9

1. Yes, I do.
2. Do you like singing?
3. No, I don't.

19.10

1. Yes, **I do**.
2. No, **I don't**.
3. **Do you like** playing the piano?
4. **No**, I don't.
5. Do you like **reading**?

19.11

1. No, I don't.
2. No, I don't.
3. Yes, I do.
4. Yes, I do.

19.12

Do you have hobbies?
Yes, I do.
I **love** reading books
and skateboarding, too.

Do you like playing **tennis**?
Yes, I do.
I love **playing** tennis
and playing **soccer**, too.

Do you **enjoy** singing?
Yes, I do.
I love **singing** songs,
and I love **dancing**, too.

21

21.1

1. watch
2. sock
3. skirt
4. shorts
5. pants
6. T-shirt
7. hat
8. dress
9. purse
10. baseball cap
11. jeans
12. shoe
13. boot
14. glasses
15. shirt
16. bag
17. jacket

21.2
1 glasses 2 T-shirt 3 shoe
4 skirt 5 purse

21.3
1 It's a **watch**. 2 It's a **shirt**.
3 They're **jeans**. 4 It's a **dress**.
5 It's a **jacket**. 6 They're **shorts**.

21.4
1 A 2 B 3 A 4 B 5 A

21.5
We're at a **party**,
so let's all **dance** and play.
What a fun **party**
for Ben's birthday!

Andy's **wearing** his
favorite **T-shirt**,
and Sara has
a beautiful **skirt**.

21.6
1 I'm wearing a jacket.
2 I'm wearing a hat.
3 I'm wearing a watch.
4 I'm wearing boots.
5 I'm wearing pants.

21.7
1 shirt
2 baseball cap
3 jeans
4 shorts
5 dress

21.8
1 Yes, I am.
2 Are you wearing a watch?
3 No, I'm not.

21.9
1 No, I'm not.
2 No, I'm not.
3 Yes, I am.

21.10
1 **What** clean shoes!
2 **What** dirty jeans!
3 **What a** nice hat!
4 **What a** colorful bag!
5 **What a** nice skirt!

21.11
1 What dirty socks!
2 What lovely pants!
3 What lovely shorts!
4 What a beautiful dress!

22

22.1
1. seagull
2. ship
3. surf
4. jellyfish
5. fly a kite
6. sand
7. play soccer
8. bucket
9. shovel
10. listen to music
11. drink juice
12. eat ice cream
13. fish
14. swim in the ocean
15. run on the beach
16. read a book
17. throw a ball
18. shell

22.2
1. seagull
2. shell
3. sand
4. ship

22.3

22.4
1. A
2. B
3. B
4. B
5. A
6. B
7. B

22.5
1. **He isn't** swimming.
2. **He's** listening to music.
3. **She isn't** drinking juice.
4. **She isn't** surfing.
5. **He's** flying a kite.
6. **She's** running.

22.6
1. She's **drinking** juice.
2. She's **surfing**.

3 He's **playing** soccer.
4 She's **reading** a book.
5 He's **listening** to music.

22.7
1 No, he isn't.
2 Yes, he is.
3 No, she isn't.
4 Yes, she is.

22.8
1 No, he isn't.
2 No, she isn't.
3 Yes, she is.

23

23.1
1 pie
2 cake
3 fries
4 candy
5 burger
6 orange
7 salad
8 rice
9 sausages
10 chocolate
11 noodles
12 drinks
13 fruit
14 juice
15 water
16 lemonade

23.2
1 fruit
2 drinks
3 cake
4 candy

23.3
1 juice
2 orange
3 noodles
4 sausages
5 rice
6 drinks
7 chocolate
8 pie

23.4
1 I'd like some fries, please.
2 I'd like some lemonade, please.
3 I'd like a burger, please.
4 I'd like some water, please.

23.5
1 I'd like **some** juice, please.
2 I'd like **some** rice, please.
3 I'd like **an** orange, please.
4 I'd like **a** burger, please.
5 I'd like **some** noodles, please.

23.6
1 No, thank you.
2 Yes, please.
3 Yes, I would.
4 No, I wouldn't.

23.7
1 breakfast
2 milk
3 egg
4 bread
5 lunch
6 meatball

7 pasta
8 dinner
9 rice
10 beans
11 fish
12 potatoes
13 chicken
14 peas

23.8
1 Fish and beans.
2 Milk and bread.
3 Meat and potatoes.
4 Chicken and peas.
5 Meatballs and rice.

23.9
1 Fish and potatoes.
2 What's for dinner?
3 Pasta and meatballs.

24

24.1
1 boy
2 girl
3 baby
4 woman
5 women
6 person
7 people
8 child/kid
9 children/kids
10 man
11 men

24.2
1 A
2 A
3 B

24.3
1 children
2 men
3 girl
4 woman
5 boy

24.4
1 man
2 kids
3 baby
4 boy

24.5
1 A
2 B
3 A
4 A
5 B

24.6
1 Is this Kim's ball?
2 Is this Nick's cat?
3 Is this Amy's book?
4 Is this Lucy's computer?
5 Is this Maria's jacket?

24.7
1 Ann
2 Matt
3 Kim
4 Sam
5 Andy

24.8

24.9
1. It's his. 2. It's ours. 3. It's yours.
4. It's theirs.

24.10
1. It's **his**. 2. It's **ours**.
3. It's **mine**. 4. It's **yours**.
5. It's **theirs**. 6. It's **hers**.
7. It's **ours**.

25

25.1
1. I get up.
2. I make my bed.
3. I eat breakfast.
4. I brush my teeth.
5. I walk to school.
6. I study English.
7. I eat lunch.
8. I go home.
9. I call my friend.
10. I go swimming.
11. I eat dinner.
12. I go to sleep.

25.2
1. I go home. 2. I get up.
3. I eat dinner. 4. I go swimming.
5. I study English.

25.3
1. I call my friend.
2. I walk to school.
3. I go to sleep.
4. I brush my teeth.
5. I eat lunch.

25.4
1. It's ten o'clock.
2. It's five o'clock.
3. It's one o'clock.
4. It's six o'clock.
5. It's four o'clock.
6. It's nine o'clock.
7. It's three o'clock.
8. It's eleven o'clock.

223

25.5

1 In the afternoon
2 In the evening   3 At night

25.6

1 I walk to school in the **morning**.
2 I eat dinner in the **evening**.
3 I go home in the **afternoon**.
4 I go to sleep at **night**.
5 I make my bed in the **morning**.

25.7

1 **When do you** get up?
2 I eat dinner **in** the evening.
3 I go to sleep **at** eight o'clock.
4 I go home at **four o'clock**.
5 I brush my teeth in the **morning** and at night.

25.8

1 We walk to school.
2 She calls her friend.
3 He brushes his teeth.
4 They eat dinner.
5 I go home.

25.9

1 Tuesday   2 Wednesday
3 Thursday   4 Friday
5 Saturday   6 Sunday

25.10

1 I go swimming **on** Tuesdays.
2 I call my friend **on** Fridays.
3 I eat lunch **at** twelve o'clock.

25.11

1 I don't.   2 I don't.   3 So do I.

Acknowledgments

The publisher would like to thank:

Ankita Awasthi Tröger for administrative assistance; Elizabeth Blakemore for editorial assistance; Laura Gardner for design assistance; Christine Stroyan, Kayla Dugger, Lori Hand, and Laura Caddell for proofreading; Christine Stroyan for audio script management and recording; and ID Audio for audio recording and production.

All images © Dorling Kindersley. For further information, visit **www.dkimages.com**.